TITLE

THE JESUS FILES

CONTRIBUTORS

AUTHOR: CARINE MACKENZIE
ILLUSTRATOR: FRED APPS

The Jesus Files

This book was given to: ....

Date: ....

From: ....

Scripture Verse:
'Believe in the Lord Jesus Christ
and you shall be saved.'
Acts 16:31

Contents

PURPOSE: Find out what you want to read and go straight there!

Chapter Title		Page Number

God's story

SCRIPTURE LOCATION: Matthew; Mark; Luke; John

THEME: What this book is about

History

The Lord Jesus Christ is the most important character of history. The word 'History' means 'His Story' – God's story, the story of Jesus, the Son of God and the Son of Man. It is important that we know about him but vital that we know him personally.

Jesus, the World and the Bible

He came to this world as a person so that we 'may have life, and have it to the full,' John 10.10. Jesus, God's Son came to bring the good news of the Gospel to us. 'Christ died for sins once for all, the righteous for the unrighteous to bring you to God,' 1 Peter 3:18. We learn about Jesus mostly in the four books of the Bible called the Gospels. These were written by Matthew, Mark, Luke and John. They tell of Jesus' life and death. Each gives different details and insights to the life and ministry of Christ.

The Jesus Files tells you about

The birth of Jesus: pages 8-13; His miracles: pages 24-25; 28-29; 80-83; His teaching: pages 16-17; 32-33; 84-87; His death: pages 48-59; 78-79; 108-109; His resurrection: pages 60-61; 110-111; His ascension: pages 64-65; His coming again: pages 66-67.

Focus, character, case Studies

To learn more you will be referred to special focus studies on aspects of Jesus' life and ministry. The character studies look at some of the friends and enemies who feature in Jesus' life. The case studies look in more detail at the birth, death and resurrection of Jesus Christ.

Scripture location, theme and link back

Scripture location and themes are given at the start of every story file. In the focus, character and case studies instead of a theme there is a link back section which will remind you of where to find stories to back up the teaching in that section.

Extra features

These include a study section and bible data answer section. The study section gives ideas for stories that you can read in the files if you want to study a particular subject. The bible data questions are found throughout the book. These will get you studying the bible for yourself and discovering all sorts of fascinating information. The bible data answer section gives you a summary of all the answers to these questions. On pages 68-69 you will find a map of Palestine and the surrounding areas and on pages 118-119 there is a general index which should help you find any information you need.

Jesus and you

Jesus' life is the most amazing: one that affects each person. The Bible tells us that if everything he did was written down, the world itself could not contain all the books that should be written. Read on and find out more about Jesus the Saviour. Pray that you would not only know about Jesus but that you would know him and love him.

Carine Mackenzie
Author

The birth announcement

SCRIPTURE LOCATION: Matthew 1; Luke 1

THEME: Jesus the Saviour

Mary was a young Jewish woman who lived in Nazareth in Galilee. She was engaged to be married to Joseph.

One day the angel Gabriel, God's messenger, came to Mary with startling news. First of all he greeted her, 'Hail to you. You are highly favoured. The Lord is with you.' Mary was anxious. She could not understand why the angel was speaking to her like this.

'Don't be afraid, Mary,' the angel added, 'God is pleased with you. You will give birth to a son. You will call him Jesus. He shall be a great king, the Son of the Highest.'

'How can that happen to me?' Mary asked, 'I am not married yet.'

'The Holy Spirit's power shall come upon you. The holy child to whom you shall give birth will be the Son of God.'

Gabriel also told her that her cousin Elizabeth, whom everyone thought was too old, was expecting a baby soon. 'With God nothing is impossible,' he said.

Mary believed these amazing things. 'May what happens to me be according to your Word,' she said.

The angel left. Mary went to visit her cousin Elizabeth in the hill country of Judea. As soon as Mary entered the house, the baby inside Elizabeth, moved vigorously. Elizabeth called out loudly, 'Blessed are you among women and blessed is your child.' Elizabeth knew about Mary's baby. She also knew that the baby was very special. God the Holy Spirit had told her and she believed.

Mary praised God in a beautiful song of love to God her Saviour. 'My soul magnifies the Lord and my spirit has rejoiced in God my Saviour.'

In this amazing way the most important birth announcement ever was made. God had sent his Son Christ Jesus to the world to be the Saviour he had promised long ago. After staying with Elizabeth for about three months, Mary returned to Nazareth.

When Joseph learned that Mary was expecting a baby, he was naturally rather upset. An angel reassured him in a dream. 'Do not be afraid to take Mary as your wife. The baby has been formed by the power of God the Holy Spirit. She will give birth to a son and you will call him Jesus for he shall save his people from their sins.'

The prophet Isaiah had said long ago that God's promised Messiah (chosen Saviour) would be born of a virgin. Joseph was happy to marry Mary then. They set up their home in Nazareth where Joseph was a carpenter.

INFORMATION SPOT

For more information on the birth of Jesus turn to pages 76-77 and page 106. To find out more about Mary turn to pages 94-95. To look up the location of Nazareth and Judea on the map turn to pages 68-69.

FILE 001/JESUS

The name Jesus means Saviour. Another name given to Jesus was 'Immanuel' which means 'God with us.' Jesus is truly human and truly God.

The birth of Jesus Christ

SCRIPTURE LOCATION: Luke 2

THEME: Jesus is worshipped

Caesar Augustus, the Roman Emperor, passed a law that everyone in the Empire should be taxed. Each man had to return to his hometown to register and pay the tax.

Joseph belonged to the family of David, so he had to go to Bethlehem, the City of David, to be taxed. Mary, his wife, had to go with him even though her baby was due very soon.

The town of Bethlehem was very busy with other visitors like Joseph and Mary. The town was so busy that there was no room in the inn for Joseph and Mary to find a bed for the night. They were allowed to take shelter in the stable.

That night Mary's baby was born. Mary wrapped her baby in swaddling clothes, like a very tight shawl and laid him to sleep in a manger, which usually held straw for the animals.

That night out in the countryside near Bethlehem, shepherds were watching over their flocks as usual. Suddenly an angel of the Lord appeared to them. The sky lit up with the glory of the Lord. The shepherds were so afraid.

'Do not be afraid,' the angel said, 'I bring good news to you. Today in the City of David, the Saviour has been born. He is Christ the Lord. You will find this baby wrapped in swaddling clothes, lying in a manger.'

Then many angels joined him, and they all praised God, 'Glory to God in the Highest, and on earth peace, good will to all men.'

When the angels returned to heaven, the shepherds said to one another, 'Let's go up to Bethlehem and see for ourselves the wonderful thing the Lord has told us.'

So they hurried to Bethlehem and found Mary and Joseph and the baby lying in the manger, exactly as the angels had told them.

The shepherds passed on this great news to everyone they met. 'The Saviour, Christ the Lord, has been born in Bethlehem,' they exclaimed. All who heard the news were amazed. Mary herself was amazed at what the shepherds told her and she often thought about it afterwards.

The shepherds returned to their work in the field glorifying and praising God for all the things that they had heard from the angels and then seen with their own eyes.

INFORMATION SPOT

For more information on Jesus the Saviour turn to pages 92-93. Look up the location of Bethlehem on the map on pages 68-69.

FILE 002/PLACE OF BIRTH

Bethlehem was a small, unimportant town. The humility of the Lord Jesus is shown to us in his becoming a person like us and in the poor and lowly circumstances of his birth.

Visiting the Temple

SCRIPTURE LOCATION: Luke 2

THEME: Jesus the Saviour

It was the Jewish law, that when the first baby boy was born in a family, he was to be called 'Holy to the Lord.' The parents had to present a sacrifice in the temple in Jerusalem. When Jesus was eight days old, Mary and Joseph made the journey of about four miles, to the temple at Jerusalem. Those who could afford it presented a lamb but Joseph and Mary were poor so they brought a pair of turtledoves or two young pigeons.

On the same day that Jesus was brought to the temple, the Holy Spirit prompted an old man called Simeon to be there too. He was upright and holy and was waiting for Christ, the Saviour that God had promised, to come. He had been told by God that he would not die until he had seen the Lord's anointed one, Jesus Christ.

When he saw Mary and Joseph with the baby Jesus, Simeon knew that at last he was looking at the Saviour.

He took the baby Jesus in his arms and praised God. 'Lord, now let your servant die in peace according to your Word,' he said, 'for my eyes have seen your salvation, which you have prepared to save both Jews and Gentiles.'

Joseph and Mary were amazed at the words spoken by Simeon. Simeon blessed them and spoke particularly to Mary. 'This child,' he said 'is come as a Saviour for many in Israel, but those who reject him will fall. You too will have suffering.'

Anna, an old widow of eighty-four years, lived in the temple at that time. She spent day and night fasting and praying. When she saw baby Jesus, she gave thanks to God. She spoke of him to many people who were looking for the Saviour.

She too believed that Jesus was the one promised to come to save.

Mary, Joseph and Jesus went back to Bethlehem.

INFORMATION SPOT

For more information on Jesus Christ turn to pages 72-73 and pages 74-75. To look up the location of Jerusalem on the map turn to pages 68-69.

FILE 003/THE TEMPLE

The temple in Jerusalem was the main building in the religious life of the Jewish people. Here the priests offered sacrifices for the sins of the people.

BIBLE DATA 001

Read Isaiah 9:1; Isaiah 42:6 and Isaiah 49:6. The promised Messiah would deliver Jews and Gentiles (non Jewish peoples). Who must obey Matthew 28:19?

SCRIPTURE LOCATION: Matthew 2

Visitors from the East

THEME: Jesus is worshipped

Wise men from the east came to visit Jesus. They had seen a strange star in the sky and believed this meant that the king of the Jews had been born. 'Let's go to worship him,' they said.

So they set off on their long journey to Jerusalem, straight to King Herod's palace. 'Where is the newborn king of the Jews? We have seen his star. We want to worship him.'

Herod was angry and jealous when he heard this. He summoned the chief priests and scribes. 'Where will Christ be born?' he asked. They quoted to him from the Scriptures, from the book of the prophet Micah. 'Christ will be born in Bethlehem,' they told him.

Herod passed on this information to the visitors.

'Look carefully for the young child,' he said to them, 'and tell me where he is so that I can go and worship him too.' But that was just an evil scheme.

The wise men followed the star and travelled on to Bethlehem to the house where Jesus was. There they saw the young child Jesus and Mary his mother. They fell down

and worshipped Jesus, and gave him beautiful gifts of gold, frankincense and myrrh. God warned the wise men to go home by a different route.

An angel spoke to Joseph in a dream, 'Take the young child and his mother and go quickly to Egypt. Stay there until I tell you. Herod is trying to kill the child.'

Joseph got up in the middle of the night and set off with Mary and baby Jesus to safety in Egypt.

Herod was even more angry when he realised that the wise men had not come back to report on where they had found the king of the Jews. He did a terrible thing. He sent his men out to Bethlehem and all the countryside round about and they cruelly killed all the boy babies of two years old and under. He thought he would be sure to kill baby Jesus that way. But Jesus was safe in Egypt.

After Herod died, the angel spoke to Joseph again in a dream. 'Take the young child and his mother back to Israel. The people who wanted to kill him are now dead.'

The family made the long journey back to Israel. Joseph was anxious because Herod's son was now king. Again the angel of God spoke to him in a dream, and guided him to go north and settle in Nazareth in Galilee.

INFORMATION SPOT

For more information on Christ's birth turn to pages 76-77 and 106-107. Egypt is on the map on pages 68-69.

FILE 004/HEROD

Two Herods are mentioned in the Bible, one at Jesus' birth and another at his death.

FILE 005/MYRRH AND OTHER GIFTS

Myrrh was an ointment used to anoint dead bodies. Gold is a gift fit for a King. Frankinsence is a perfume used by priests. So the gifts show us Jesus is King, a Priest to bring us to God and that he has died for his people.

At the Passover feast

SCRIPTURE LOCATION: Luke 2

THEME: Jesus' childhood

Every year Joseph and Mary would make the journey from Nazareth to the temple in Jerusalem to celebrate the Passover feast. When Jesus was twelve years old, he was old enough to go with them. They stayed in Jerusalem for several days worshipping God.

When it was time to set off for home again, Jesus stayed behind in the temple. Mary and Joseph were unaware of this and travelled on assuming that Jesus was with friends on the road to Nazareth too.

At the end of the day they began to search for him, asking all their friends and relations if they had seen Jesus. But no one had seen him. Anxiously Mary and Joseph hurried back to Jerusalem looking for Jesus all the time.

Three days later they found him in the temple, sitting with the teachers, listening to them and asking questions.

Everyone was astonished at his understanding and at the answers he gave. Mary and Joseph were amazed too when they saw what he was doing. 'Son, why have you done this to us?' Mary asked. 'Your father and I have been so worried looking for you.'

'Why were you looking for me?' Jesus replied. 'Did you not know that I have to do my Father's business?' He meant that he had to be learning about the things of God, his heavenly Father.

Mary and Joseph did not understand but Mary remembered his words and often thought about them.

Jesus left the teachers in the temple and went back to Nazareth with his parents. He was a dutiful and obedient son, honouring his mother and father, as God's commandments require. Jesus grew up like other boys except that he had no sin in him at all.

As he became a man, he became even wiser. God was pleased with his life and all who met him realised there was something very special about him.

Jesus worked in the family carpentry business making wooden articles. At the age of thirty years, he began his public ministry.

INFORMATION SPOT

For more information on Jesus' teaching turn to pages 84-85. To find out about another time that Jesus went to Jerusalem turn to pages 46-47.

FILE 005/THE PASSOVER FEAST

The Passover Feast began when the children of Israel were slaves in Egypt. They were told to paint the blood of a lamb on their doorposts. The angel of death then passed over them. The feast reminded them of that great escape. It was held every year.

Jesus' baptism

SCRIPTURE LOCATION: Matthew 3; John 1

THEME: Jesus the sacrifice

When Jesus was thirty years old, he started the great work that God had sent him to do. He travelled from Galilee to the river Jordan, near Bethabara. Many people came here to hear a special preacher called John, Elizabeth's son. He told the people, 'You must repent, turn from your sins to God.'

He also told them 'Someone far more important than me will speak to you soon.' This 'more important person' was Jesus.

One day when Jesus was walking towards John, John turned to the crowd and said 'Behold the Lamb of God that takes away the sin of the world.'

John realised that Jesus was the Son of God. The listeners would all be familiar with a lamb being used as a sacrifice for sins. John knew that Jesus was to be the great sacrifice for sin.

Many people turned from their sins when they heard John preaching. They were baptised in the river Jordan. Baptism is an outward sign of the washing away of sins.

Jesus also asked to be baptised, John was surprised, 'How can I baptise you?' he asked, 'You should baptise me.'

John knew that Jesus had no sins to be washed away. He did not need to repent. But Jesus insisted. He was baptised just like other people who loved the Lord God. It was an example to others and shows us that he was fully man. When he came up from the river Jordan, God the Holy Spirit came down from heaven in the form of a dove and rested on Jesus.

God the Father spoke from heaven, 'This is my beloved Son, in whom I am well pleased.' God was pleased with what Jesus had done.

John knew that Jesus was to become more important.

INFORMATION SPOT

For more information on John the Baptist turn to page 72 and pages 96-97. The River Jordan is on the map on pages 68-69.

FILE 006/TRINITY

The Holy Spirit is the third person in the Trinity. In this story we see all three members of the Trinity - God the Son, God the Father and God the Holy Spirit.

BIBLE DATA 002

Read Hebrews 4:15; 1 John 1:8 and Romans 3:23. Who does the Bible tell us are sinners and who are not?

Desert temptation

SCRIPTURE LOCATION: Matthew 4; Luke 4

THEME: Jesus suffers

After his baptism, Jesus was led by the Holy Spirit in the wilderness – a lonely, barren desert. He was alone there for forty days with no food or company. He must have felt very tired and hungry.

The Devil spoke to him, tempting him to do wrong. 'If you are the Son of God,' he said, 'make these stones into bread.' Jesus did not give in to the temptation; he answered the Devil by quoting a verse from the Bible. 'It is written,' he said, '"Man shall not live by bread alone, but by every word that God says."'

The Devil tried again. He took Jesus up to one of the high towers on the temple at Jerusalem, 'If you are the Son of God,' he said, 'throw yourself down to the ground. Doesn't the Bible say that God will send an angel to take care of you?'

Again Jesus quoted the Bible to answer the wicked temptation of the Devil. 'It is written,' he said, '"You shall not tempt the Lord your God."'

Once more the Devil tried to make Jesus sin. He took him up to a high mountain and showed him all the kingdoms of the world. How good they looked.

'I will give all these lands to you,' said the Devil, 'if you will just bow down and worship me.'

'Go away, Satan,' answered Jesus, 'It is written, "Worship the Lord your God and serve only him."'

The Devil could do no more. He left Jesus alone. Angels came to attend to Jesus and to comfort him.

INFORMATION SPOT

For more information on Jesus and the Bible turn to pages 70-71.

FILE 007/THE DEVIL

The Devil is a name for Satan, the angel who rebelled against God. Jesus describes the Devil in John 8:44 'There is no truth in him.'

FILE 008/SCRIPTURES

Jesus read and learned the Scripture of the Old Testament. When he answered the Devil he quoted three times from Deuteronomy. He knew and sang the Psalms. Quoting scripture is a good example to follow. When you suffer from temptation turn to God's word for help.

BIBLE DATA 003

When we are tempted we want to sin. What does the Bible say about temptation? Read Mark 14:38; Luke 22:40 and 1 Corinthians 10:13 to find out what it is.

Jesus and his disciples

SCRIPTURE LOCATION: Matthew 10; Mark 1; Luke 5; John 2

THEME: Jesus preaches and teaches

Jesus started to preach the good news of God in Galilee. 'The kingdom of God is near. Repent and believe the Gospel.'

One day by the Sea of Galilee Jesus met a fisherman called Andrew. Andrew realised that Jesus was the Christ (Messiah) the Saviour of sinners, whom God had promised to send. Andrew hurried to tell his brother Simon and then took Simon to see Jesus. Jesus spoke kindly to Simon and gave him another name. He called him 'Peter' which means 'a stone'.

'Come and follow me,' Jesus said to Andrew and Peter, ' and I will make you fishers of men.' They immediately left their fishing nets and followed Jesus. They were his first disciples.

A little further on he met two other fishermen, James and his brother John. They were in their boat mending their nets. When Jesus called them, they left their father Zebedee in the boat with the hired servants and followed Jesus.

The following day Jesus wanted to go to Galilee. He found Philip, who was from Bethsaida, the same town as Andrew and Peter. 'Follow me,' Jesus said to Philip.

Philip found Nathanael (also known as Bartholomew). 'We have found the one that Moses and the prophets wrote about,' Philip exclaimed, 'Jesus of Nazareth, the son of Joseph.'

'Can anything good come from Nazareth?' asked Nathanael.

'Come and see for yourself,' replied Philip.

When Jesus saw Nathanael coming towards him he said, 'Here comes an honest man – a true son of Israel.'

'How do you know what I am like?' Nathanael demanded.

'I saw you under the fig tree, before Philip called you,' answered Jesus.

'You are the Son of God,' admitted Nathanael, 'the King of Israel.'

Nathanael became a disciple too.

Levi was a tax collector. One day he was sitting in his collector's booth, Jesus came up to him and said, 'Follow me,' Levi obeyed at once. He became one of the disciples. His name was changed to Matthew.

INFORMATION SPOT

For more information on Peter turn to pages 98-99. For information on Judas Iscariot turn to pages 104-105. Bethsaida is on the map on pages 68-69. For a full list of all twelve disciples read Luke 6:12-16.

FILE 09/THE CHRIST

Christ in Greek means 'Anointed One'. In Hebrew this is 'Messiah'. God had promised a Messiah – a Saviour for his people. Jesus fulfilled these prophecies.

The first miracle

SCRIPTURE LOCATION: John 2

THEME: Jesus is powerful

Jesus and his mother, Mary, were invited to a wedding in the village of Cana in Galilee. The disciples, Jesus' special friends, were among the many guests.

During the feast the servants discovered that the wine was finished. This was quite a problem for the groom and for the family who were arranging the wedding feast. Mary came to Jesus, 'They have no wine left,' she told him.

Jesus answered, 'Woman, what can I do about that? My time has not come yet.'

But Mary said to the servants, 'Do whatever Jesus tells you.'

Now in the room there were six big stone water pots used for washing. Each could hold twenty to thirty gallons of water.

'Fill these water pots with water,' Jesus told the servants.

The men filled them up to the brim.

'Now take a cupful to the master of the feast.'

The servants did this and when the master of the feast drank some of the wine, he thought it was the best wine he had ever tasted.

He had not been aware of the problem and did not know where the wine had come from. He called the bridegroom over and congratulated him on the good wine.

'Most people give the best wines first,' he said. 'Then they bring out the poorer wines when everyone has had their fill. However you have kept the good wine until now.'

Mary and the servants who filled the water pots knew that Jesus had changed the water into wine. This was the first miracle that Jesus did. It showed his power and glory. The disciples believed that he was truly the Christ.

INFORMATION SPOT

For more information on other miracles turn to pages 80-83. To find out more about Mary turn to pages 94-95.

FILE 010/ CANA IN GALILEE

Cana is mentioned three times in the New Testament. As well as the wedding that was held at Cana, Nathanael, one of the disciples came from Cana, and Jesus healed the son of a royal official there. Cana is on the map on pages 68-69.

FILE 011/A WEDDING

A wedding feast in those days would have lasted for several days, not just one meal. The wine would have been the responsibility of the bridegroom. He would have been very upset and embarrassed if the wine had run out. Jesus showed his power over creation and also his concern for the people with this miracle.

Jesus the preacher

SCRIPTURE LOCATION: Matthew 5; John 3 and 4

THEME: Jesus preaches and teaches

Jesus was an amazing preacher. Crowds followed him to hear his teachings. He preached to large crowds in many different places but he would also take time to speak to one person, explaining an important truth.

Nicodemus, a Jewish ruler, came to Jesus one night, with some questions. 'Unless you are born again,' Jesus told him, 'you can never get into the kingdom of God.' Nicodemus could not understand this. Jesus explained to him the new life which God the Holy Spirit gives. Jesus compared the work of the Holy Spirit to the wind. We cannot tell where the wind comes from or where it will go next, but we see its effects. The Holy Spirit's work is like that.

Jesus told Nicodemus about God's great love for his people and his plan of salvation for needy sinners. 'God loved the world so much,' he told him, 'that he gave his only Son that anyone who believes in him shall not perish but have eternal life.' What good news for Nicodemus and us.

Jesus had an important conversation with a Samaritan woman who had come to a well to draw water. It was the middle of the day and Jesus asked the woman for a drink and so the conversation started. He told her how he was the source of true satisfaction. He confronted her with the sad facts of her own immoral lifestyle. He explained the importance of worshipping God in spirit and in truth. The place did not matter. He told her plainly that he was the promised Messiah, the Christ.

The woman left her water pots and went back to the city to tell everyone, 'Come and meet a man who told me everything I ever did. Is not this the Christ?'

While sitting on a mountainside Jesus preached to many people, including his disciples. He gave a surprising list of those truly happy and blessed – the poor in spirit, those who mourn, the meek and lowly, the kind, peaceable and even those who suffer because they are good.

Jesus spoke too about keeping the law, not just outwardly, but with right motives.

Jesus taught about prayer and even gave a short simple prayer as an example.

Jesus told us to pray to God who cares for us just like a father cares for his children.

If a child asks his father for a piece of bread, he will not give him a stone instead. God is much more loving than any father.

Many people were astonished at Jesus' teachings. He taught with great authority.

INFORMATION SPOT

For more information on Jesus and prayer turn to pages 74-75. To find out more about what he taught turn to pages 86-87.

FILE 012/PREACHING

Jesus preached the word of God in many different places. People still preach about Jesus today. It is the method God has chosen to save his people. We are told the good news that Christ died to save his people from their sins. This is to be preached to everyone.

On the Sea of Galilee

SCRIPTURE LOCATION: Matthew 8, 14; Mark 4, 6

THEME: Jesus is powerful

One evening Jesus said to his disciples, 'Let's cross over to the other side of the Sea.'

While they were crossing Jesus fell asleep in the boat because he was tired. Soon a great storm blew up. The wind howled and the waves came over the sides of the boat. The disciples were frightened. They woke Jesus up, 'Lord, save us.'

Jesus said to them, 'Why are you so afraid? How weak your faith is.'

Jesus then spoke to the wind and to the sea, 'Peace, be still.'

The wind stopped blowing. The sea became calm. The disciples were astonished at the power Jesus had over the wind and sea.

Another evening, after a busy day, the disciples were told by Jesus to sail across the lake. Jesus did not go with them. He wanted to be alone to pray to God his Father.

As the disciples were rowing across the big lake, it became dark. The wind blew strongly against them. It was very rough and stormy. The little boat was tossed about by the waves. Some time between three and six o'clock in the morning the disciples saw someone walking on the waves. They were terrified, 'It's a ghost!' one exclaimed.

But then they heard the voice of Jesus, saying, 'It is I, do not be afraid.'

Peter shouted back, 'Lord, if it is really you, tell me to come on the water to meet you.'

'Come,' Jesus replied.

So Peter climbed over the side of the boat and began to walk towards Jesus. Peter looked at the tossing waves and became scared. Then he began to sink.

He shouted to Jesus in fear, 'Lord, save me.'

Jesus reached out and caught hold of Peter. 'Why did you doubt?' he asked him.

They both got into the boat and immediately the wind died down. The disciples were amazed. They worshipped Jesus saying, 'Truly you are the Son of God.' This amazing miracle convinced the disciples that the man Jesus was truly God as well.

INFORMATION SPOT

For more information on Peter turn to pages 98-99.

FILE 013/SEA OF GALILEE

The Sea of Galilee is 211 metres below sea level. Strong winds often sweep between the surrounding hills causing extremely sudden and violent storms. Jesus was often in the towns and villages around the Sea of Galilee – Capernaum, Bethsaida and the Sea of Galilee are on the map on pages 68-69.

BIBLE DATA 004

Name another person who was certain that Jesus was the Son of God. Look up pages 56-57 or read Mark 15:33-39.

Jairus' daughter

SCRIPTURE LOCATION: Matthew 9; Mark 5; Luke 8

THEME: Jesus is powerful

Jairus was an important man in the Jewish synagogue. He came to Jesus one day to ask him to heal his daughter who was dying. She was only twelve years old.

Jairus made his way towards Jesus and fell down before him, 'Please come to my house, my little daughter is so ill. I am afraid she will die.'

Jesus set off with Jairus towards his house. With so many people crowding round it was difficult to make progress. Suddenly Jesus stopped and said, 'Who touched me?'

Everyone denied it. 'It wasn't me.' 'I didn't touch you either.' 'No, not me.'

Peter and his friends said to Jesus, 'Master, the crowd is so close. You should not be surprised that someone touched you.'

'Somebody has touched me deliberately,' replied Jesus. 'I know that power has gone out from me.'

Just then a woman came out of the crowd. She was afraid and trembling. She told Jesus that she had touched him and had been healed immediately. She had been bleeding for twelve years and had spent all her money on doctor's bills. No medicine had helped her. When she saw Jesus she thought, 'If only I could touch the hem of his garment, I might be healed.'

Jesus comforted and encouraged the woman, 'Your faith has made you well, go in peace,' he said.

Just as he was speaking, one of Jairus' servants came hurrying up with bad news. 'Your daughter is dead,' he told Jairus, 'do not trouble the Master any more.'

'Do not be afraid,' said Jesus, 'just believe and she will be made better.'

Large crowds of people were standing around Jairus' house weeping loudly. When Jesus told them to be quiet because the girl was not dead but sleeping the crowd laughed. So Jesus sent them all out and only allowed Peter, James and John and Jairus and his wife to come into the room with him. He took the little girl's hand and said, 'Little girl, get up.'

Immediately her life revived and she got up out of bed, 'Give her something to eat now,' Jesus ordered.

Her parents were amazed and overjoyed. Jesus the Creator of life, had power to heal the sick woman and to restore to life the little girl.

INFORMATION SPOT

For more information on miracles of healing turn to pages 80-81.

FILE 014/MOURNERS

Jewish families had a period of mourning after a death. They made a great noise of wailing to show distress. If you were from a wealthy family sometimes professional mourners were hired.

Parable of the sower

SCRIPTURE LOCATION: Matthew 13

THEME: Jesus preaches and teaches

Many people flocked to hear Jesus preach. One day Jesus got into a boat on the Sea of Galilee and sat down, while the people stood on the shore. He told them a story, or parable.

A farmer went out to sow some seed in his field – up and down scattering the seed to left and right. Some seeds fell on the pathway. The birds soon came and ate them up.

Some seed fell on shallow stony ground. They grew up quickly. Soon green shoots appeared through the earth, but when the sun shone brightly and the weather became very hot, the shoots withered and died. The roots could not go down far enough to get moisture.

Other seeds fell among thorns and weeds. These seeds grew but so did the thorns and they soon choked the good corn.

Some seeds landed on good ground with no stones, or thorns or weeds. This seed grew well and at harvest-time the farmer reaped thirty times as much seed as he planted or even sixty or one hundred times as much.

What was the meaning of the parable? Jesus explained it to his disciples.

The seed is like the Word of God. God sends his Word in different ways to men and women, and boys and girls. Some people hear God's Word but soon the devil makes them think of something else and forget about the Bible. That is like the seed, which fell on the pathway, stolen by the birds.

Other people hear God's Word and listen to it gladly at first. It seems to have an effect on their lives. But when trouble comes their interest in God's Word withers away. They are like the seed on the stony ground, which has no deep root.

The seed among the thorns was like the person who hears the Word of God but riches and pleasures are more important to them and soon choke any interest in the Bible. How wonderful that some people hear God's Word and love it and obey it. Their lives are made new. They are like the seed in the good ground. Their lives are fruitful.

INFORMATION SPOT

For more information on what Jesus taught turn to pages 84–85 and 86-87.

FILE 015/LISTENERS AND REACTION

Here is the list of reactions by the people in the story. Some believed; some mocked; some ignored. This is the same today. Which of these reactions do you have?

BIBLE DATA/005

In Matthew 17:5 who tells us to listen to Jesus? In James 1:19 what are we to be quick to do and slow to do?

Feeding five thousand

SCRIPTURE LOCATION: Matthew 14 and 15; John 6

THEME: Jesus is powerful

When Jesus heard the tragic news that John the Baptist had been killed, he wanted to get away alone quietly for a while. So he sailed across the Sea of Galilee to find a quiet spot.

But someone had seen him go with the disciples. So many people wanted to listen to Jesus. They walked round the lake to the place where Jesus went by boat.

When Jesus saw this large crowd of over 5000 people, he took pity on them and gave up his time of rest to speak with them and teach them many things.

When the evening came the disciples said, 'this place is very quiet. It is getting late. Send the people away to buy food.'

'They do not need to go away,' said Jesus. 'You give them something to eat.'

Jesus knew what he would do already.

'There is a boy here,' said Andrew, 'who has five small loaves of bread and two small fishes. But how will they feed so many people?'

'Make the people sit down on the grass,' ordered Jesus.

Jesus took the loaves and gave thanks to God for the food. He then broke the loaves and fishes into pieces and handed them to his disciples. They passed the pieces to the people sitting on the grass in groups of fifty or one hundred. Jesus kept on breaking the food into pieces until everyone had as much as they could eat.

Jesus, the Creator of all food had multiplied the loaves and fishes to feed over five thousand people. Afterwards the disciples cleared up what was left. They filled twelve big baskets with the leftovers. Jesus had provided more than enough.

On another occasion Jesus fed a big crowd of over 4000 people who had been with him for three days listening to his teaching. 'How many loaves do you have?' he asked the disciples. 'Seven,' they replied, 'and a few fishes.'

After giving thanks to God for the food, he broke it – handed the pieces to the disciples, who passed it on. They all ate till they were full. Afterwards seven baskets of leftovers were gathered up.

INFORMATION SPOT

For more information on miracles turn to pages 82-83. To find out more about John the Baptist turn to pages 96-97.

FILE 016/BIBLE TIME FOOD

Grains: wheat, barley, millet and spelt. These could be made into flour.

Cucumber and lentils, figs, almonds, pomegranates, melons and olives were grown in the area.

Mint, dill and cumin are herbs that are mentioned in Matthew 23:23.

Sea and fresh water fish were eaten. The fish would be salted, in order to preserve it, and then transported to other towns and cities such as Jerusalem.

Preparing the way

SCRIPTURE LOCATION: Matthew 16 and 17

THEME: Jesus is God's Son

Many people who met Jesus, believed on him when they heard his teaching and saw the miracles. They followed him and wanted to learn more.

Others did not believe that he was anyone special. Some were angry and saw Jesus as a threat to their own position of power.

One day Jesus and his disciples were talking together. 'Whom do people say that I am?' Jesus asked.

'Some people think you are John the Baptist, or Elijah or Jeremiah, or another great prophet came back to life,' they replied.

Then he asked more personally, 'But who do you think I am?'

Peter spoke up. 'You are the Christ,' he said, 'the Son of the Living God.'

God the Father had revealed this amazing fact to Peter.

From then on Jesus warned his disciples that he would soon have to go to Jerusalem. There he would suffer greatly and be killed, but would rise again on the third day.

Jesus took Peter, James and John up a mountain to pray. While they watched, Jesus' appearance changed. His face shone as bright as light. They saw Moses and Elijah talking with him. Then a bright cloud covered them and they heard God's voice saying about Jesus, 'This is my beloved Son and I am very pleased with him. Listen to him.'

Peter, James and John fell to the ground, afraid. Jesus came over and touched them. 'Get up,' he said, 'don't be afraid.'

When they looked up they saw that Jesus was alone.

As they were going down the mountain, Jesus told them not to tell anyone what they had seen until after he had risen from the dead. Jesus was again warning them of what was to come.

INFORMATION SPOT

For more information on the resurrection turn to pages 60-61 and pages 110-111. To find out more about Jesus turn to pages 72-73 and 88-91.

FILE 017/GOD'S WORDS

The story of Jesus on the mountain is called the transfiguration. God's words at the transfiguration are similar to those he spoke at Jesus' baptism. Read Psalm 2:7 and Isaiah 42:1 to find other words that also sound like this.

BIBLE DATA 006

Read Matthew 14:1-12. Who was mistaken about the identity of Jesus?

The good neighbour

SCRIPTURE LOCATION: Luke 10

THEME: Jesus preaches and teaches

A smart lawyer posed a question to Jesus. 'Master, what shall I do to gain eternal life?'

Jesus replied with another question, 'What do you read about that in God's Word?'

The man answered, 'God's Word tells us to love God with all our heart, soul, strength and mind, and also to love our neighbour as ourselves.'

'That is correct,' said Jesus.

'But who is my neighbour?' the lawyer added.

Jesus answered with a story.

A man travelled along the dangerous road from Jerusalem to Jericho. A band of robbers pounced on him, stole his clothes, beat him up and left him for dead.

A priest was travelling along the road too. He saw the man lying battered and naked but took no notice. He passed by on the other side of the road, showing no care. Another

religious man came along, a Levite. He looked at the man but did not help either. The next on the scene was a Samaritan. Samaritans and Jewish people were not usually friends but this Samaritan took pity on the poor traveller. He bandaged his wounds and poured oil and wine on them to soothe and cleanse the sores. Then he lifted him on his donkey and took him to the nearest inn. He looked after the man there.

The next day the Samaritan had to leave but he gave money to the innkeeper. 'Look after the man. If you need more money, I will give it to you the next time I pass this way.'

Jesus asked the lawyer the question, 'Which of these three was a neighbour to the man who was attacked?'

'The one who showed kindness to him – the Samaritan,' he replied.

'You should do the same,' said Jesus.

INFORMATION SPOT

For more information on parables turn to pages 84-85. To find out the location of Samaria on the map turn to pages 68-69.

FILE 018/THE CHARACTERS

In this story it is the Samaritan who is the hero. In Jesus' time people from Samaria were despised by the Jews. However in this story the Jewish priest and the Levite are shown to be unmerciful.

FILE 019/PARABLE:

A parable is a story that Jesus used to teach people. It had a meaning that was hidden from worldly people but that was revealed to people who loved Him. Today God's Holy Spirit helps us understand God's word.

Friends in Bethany

SCRIPTURE LOCATION: Luke 10; John 11 and 12

THEME: Jesus is powerful

Jesus had friends in the town of Bethany, two sisters, Mary and Martha, and their brother, Lazarus. Sometimes Jesus came to their house for a meal. One time Martha was anxious that everything would be just right for her guest. While she was busy preparing, her sister Mary was sitting beside Jesus listening to his wise teaching. Martha was tired and cross. 'Ask my sister to help me,' she complained.

'Martha, Martha,' Jesus replied lovingly, 'you are anxious about all the work you have to do. There is one thing that is most important. Mary is doing the right thing.'

One day the sisters were both very worried, Lazarus was very ill. 'Let's send for Jesus,' they suggested, 'he will be able to help.'

Jesus received their message but he did not rush immediately to Bethany. He had greater plans. Lazarus died. By the time Jesus reached Bethany, Lazarus had been dead and buried for four days.

When Martha heard that Jesus was on his way, she ran out of the house to meet him. Mary stayed at home.

'If only you had been here,' Martha cried, 'Lazarus would not have died.'

'Your brother will rise again,' Jesus assured her.

'I know he will rise again in the resurrection at the last day,' she replied.

'I am the resurrection and the life,' Jesus said, 'He that believes in me shall live and never die. Do you believe that?'

'Yes Lord, I believe that you are the Christ, the Son of God,' Martha confessed.

She returned to the house to tell Mary that Jesus had come. Mary went to greet Jesus with the same sad message.

They took Jesus to the place where Lazarus was buried. Jesus wept there. 'Take the stone away,' Jesus ordered. Jesus prayed to God the Father, then shouted loudly, 'Lazarus come out!'

Lazarus walked out of the grave still wearing the linen grave clothes. Mary and Martha were overjoyed. Many people, who saw this miracle, believed in Jesus and became his followers.

Another day Jesus was again in another house in Bethany for supper. Martha was helping to serve. Mary came into the room with an expensive jar of ointment. She poured all of it over Jesus' feet and wiped his feet with her hair. She did this to show Jesus how much she loved him. Judas Iscariot complained at this extravagance, but Jesus was pleased with what she had done.

INFORMATION SPOT

For more information on healing miracles turn to pages 80-81 and to pages 30-31. For more information on Judas Iscariot turn to pages 104-105.

FILE 020/BELIEF IN CHRIST

It is important to believe in Christ. Martha believed that Jesus was the Son of God. Lazarus confirmed this wonderful fact and many others believed in Jesus too.

The loving father

SCRIPTURE LOCATION: Luke 15

THEME: Jesus teaches and preaches

Church leaders sometimes complained that Jesus spent time with dishonest tax collectors and other sinners. Jesus explained that it caused joy in heaven when a sinner repented of his sin and turned to God. He told a story to show how loving God is.

A father had two sons. The older son worked on his father's farm. The younger one wanted to leave home to enjoy himself. One day, he said to his father, 'Half of your money, father, will be mine one day. Can I have that money now?'

His father agreed and gave him half his wealth.

A few days later the younger son left home and travelled far away. He had plenty of money to spend on food and drink and parties. Friends flocked around him because of his money. But eventually the money was all used up. The friends disappeared. There was a shortage of food in the land. The young man was hungry, with no friends to help. He needed to find a job. A pig farmer hired him to look after the pigs. He was so hungry he could have eaten the pigs' food. But no one gave him anything.

At last he came to his senses. 'Here I am starving,' he thought, 'and the lowest servants in my father's house have plenty to eat. I will go back to my father. I will admit that I have sinned against him and against God. I will ask to be one of his servants, for I am not worthy to be his son.'

So he set off for home. When he was still a good distance from the house, he saw a figure running down the road to greet him. It was his father. The father kissed and hugged his son.

'Oh, Father,' the boy said, 'I have sinned against heaven and you, I am not worthy to be your son.'

The father called to his servants, 'Bring out the best robe. Put a ring on his hand and shoes on his feet. Prepare a special meal with a fatted calf. Let's celebrate. My son was as if dead, but now is alive. He was lost and is found.' So the party began.

The older son had been working hard in the field all day. When he came near the house, he heard the sound of music and dancing.

'What's all this noise about?' he shouted to a servant.

'It is good news,' the servant replied. 'Your brother has come home, your father has ordered a celebration.'

The older brother was so angry; he would not even go into the house. His father came out to reason with him. 'I have worked for you for years and always done what you wished. You have never even given me a party with my friends. But as soon as this boy who has wasted your money comes back, you make a grand feast.'

His father gently replied, 'Son, you are always with me and all that I have is yours. It was right for us to rejoice. Your brother was as good as dead and is now alive. He was lost and is now found.'

INFORMATION SPOT

The story of the loving father is sometimes called the story of the prodigal son. For more information on parables turn to pages 84-85.

FILE 021/THE LOVE OF GOD

The father in Jesus' story runs to meet his son and gives him a big hug. God loves us in the same way. He sent his son to die on the cross to save his people from their sins.

Two tax collectors

SCRIPTURE LOCATION: Luke 18 and 19

THEME: Jesus the Saviour

In Jesus' time, the tax collector was a hated figure. No one liked him because he was usually dishonest. A Pharisee belonged to a religious group who liked to keep separate from others and kept the law very strictly. Pharisees were generally respected in the community because they went to the synagogue, were experts in the law and were socially superior to others. However they could often be harsh with people and full of pride in themselves.

Jesus told a story about a tax collector and a Pharisee who went to the temple to pray.

The Pharisee was very proud of himself and thought he was very good. When he prayed he told God how good he was. 'Thank you, God, that I am not greedy or immoral or dishonest like other people. I am not like that tax collector over there. I fast twice a week. I give one tenth of all my income to you.' He was very pleased with himself.

The tax collector was quite different. He knew he was a sinner and that God was holy. He stood humbly with his head bowed and said, 'God have mercy on me, a sinner.'

This was a real prayer from the heart. Jesus tells us that this man was forgiven by God, but the Pharisee was not.

When Jesus visited Jericho he met the chief tax collector, called Zacchaeus. He was very rich because he had cheated people, making them pay too much tax. Crowds of people wanted to see Jesus that day. They lined the streets of Jericho as Jesus passed along.

Zacchaeus was quite short. He could not see over the heads of the taller people, so he ran further along the road and climbed a sycamore tree to get a good view.

Jesus looked up at him. 'Hurry down Zacchaeus,' he said, 'I want to come to your house today.'

Zacchaeus was delighted to welcome Jesus to his home. The people grumbled. Zacchaeus was not popular because he was a cheat. Meeting with Jesus changed Zacchaeus.

'Lord, I will give half of my wealth to the poor,' he told Jesus. 'If I have cheated anyone, I will give back four times as much.'

'Salvation has come to this house today,' said Jesus. 'The Son of Man came to seek and to save the lost.

44

INFORMATION SPOT

For more information on Jesus the Saviour turn to pages 92-93; the Pharisees turn to pages 102-103. Jericho is on the map on pages 68-69.

FILE 022/WHY JESUS CAME

The Son of God came to save his people from eternal punishment. This is God's plan of salvation. Jesus came to seek and to save the lost. Those who realise their need and ask for forgiveness receive eternal life in heaven.

Jesus goes to Jerusalem

SCRIPTURE LOCATION: Matthew 21, 26; Mark 11; Luke 19; John 12

THEME: Jesus is worshipped

Jesus and his disciples made the journey towards Jerusalem. When they reached the Mount of Olives, Jesus called two of his disciples. 'Go to that village over there,' he said, 'you will find a young donkey tethered there. It has never been ridden. Untie the animal and bring him to me. If anyone asks what you are doing, tell them the Lord needs this donkey.'

The two disciples found the donkey just as Jesus had described, tied outside a house. The owners asked what they were doing, but the answer, 'The Lord needs him,' satisfied them fully.

The men brought the young donkey to Jesus; they threw cloaks over it.

Jesus rode in triumph into Jerusalem on the back of the donkey. Some people laid their coats on the road. Others cut down branches from the trees nearby and spread them on the road.

The disciples began to shout and sing praises to God. People came out from Jerusalem to meet him waving branches of palm trees and crying out 'Hosanna to the Son of David. Blessed is the king that comes in the name of the Lord.'

Some church leaders were displeased to hear the shouts of praise and triumph from the disciples and others. 'Tell them to be quiet,' they told Jesus. But Jesus refused.

The next day in the temple Jesus chased away the greedy men who were using God's house as a place of business. He overturned the tables of the money-changers and the benches of those selling doves.

Little children sang praises and shouted 'Hosanna to the Son of David.' Jesus was glad to hear them. When some people complained, Jesus replied, 'Haven't you read in the Scripture, "Even little babies will praise him!"'

At evening he left the city to go out to stay in Bethany.

Two days later many church leaders met with Caiaphas, the high priest, to plot to kill Jesus. Judas Iscariot, one of the twelve disciples, came to this meeting and offered to help catch Jesus. 'What will you give me' he asked, 'if I give him over to you?'

So they agreed to give Judas Iscariot thirty pieces of silver if he would betray Jesus. From then on, he was on the alert to turn Jesus over to his enemies.

INFORMATION SPOT

For more information on the names of Jesus turn to pages 88-91. Turn to pages 12-13 to read about the first time Jesus went to Jerusalem.

FILE 023/JESUS AND THE PSALMS

Jesus quoted from Psalm 8 in reply to the people who complained that the children were praising him. Jesus would have sung the psalms and learned them. Many of the psalms speak about him – his life, his suffering and his death.

The last supper

SCRIPTURE LOCATION: Matthew 26

THEME: Jesus suffers

Jesus sent two of his disciples on ahead into Jerusalem to prepare the Passover Feast.

'You will meet a man carrying a jar of water,' Jesus said. 'He will lead you to a house. Explain to the owner that you will need a room to eat the Passover Feast. He will show you to a large upstairs room. Get everything ready there.'

They followed the instructions and in the evening Jesus arrived with the rest of the disciples.

This was a very special Passover Feast. Jesus was preparing himself and his friends for his death.

He broke the bread and handed it round. 'This is my body,' he said. Then he passed round a cup of wine. 'This is my blood. When you eat the bread and drink the wine, remember me.'

Jesus knew what Judas Iscariot was plotting. He said to the disciples, 'One of you shall betray me.'

'Lord, tell us who it is,' one of them said.

'It is the man,' replied Jesus, 'to whom I shall give this piece of food.'

He took the bread, dipped it in a dish and handed it to Judas Iscariot. Immediately Judas left the room and went out into the dark night.

Jesus spoke with the disciples for many hours, warning them of difficult times ahead. Peter boldly announced that he would never let Jesus down. Jesus sadly said, 'Before the cock crows twice you will have denied three times that you ever knew me.'

Jesus and his friends sang a psalm together before they went outside.

INFORMATION SPOT

For more information on Judas Iscariot turn to pages 104-105.

FILE 024/THE LORD'S SUPPER

At the last supper with his disciples, Jesus told them to remember his death with the symbols of his body and blood, the bread and the wine. Followers of Jesus still remember his death in this way at the communion service or the Lord's Supper.

BIBLE DATA 007

1 Corinthians 11:23-26 is about the last supper. Why should believers in Jesus take part in this special supper for the Lord? Read verse 28 it tells us that we are to do something before taking part in the Lord's supper. What is this?

Garden of Gethsemane

SCRIPTURE LOCATION: Matthew 26; John 18

THEME: Jesus suffers

Jesus and the disciples went to a garden called Gethsemane. 'Sit here,' he said, 'while I go over there to pray.'

He took Peter, James and John with him, 'I am troubled,' he said. 'Stay here and keep me company.' He went a little further on and fell down on his face and prayed to God his Father. 'Oh my Father, if it is possible let this cup be taken away from me. But may your will be done, not mine.'

When he came back to the disciples, he found them sleeping. 'Could you not watch with me for one hour?' he asked.

Jesus prayed again to God the Father. Again the disciples fell asleep. 'Are you still sleeping? Let's go now. Here comes the man who is betraying me.'

Judas knew that the garden of Gethsemane was a favourite place for Jesus. He often went there with the disciples. Judas came to the garden with a large mob of men armed with swords and other weapons. They had made a plan.

'I will point out Jesus to you by giving him a kiss,' agreed Judas.

Jesus knew what was to happen. He bravely approached the crowd.

'Who are you looking for?' he asked.

'Jesus of Nazareth,' they replied.

'I am he,' said Jesus simply.

Judas and the men were startled by Jesus' straight reply. Judas carried out the arranged plan. 'Master,' he greeted Jesus, giving him a kiss.

When the disciples saw what was happening they wanted to fight. Peter lashed out with his sword and cut off the ear of the high priest's servant. 'No more of this!' said Jesus. He touched the man's ear and it was healed immediately.

The soldiers caught hold of Jesus, tied him up and led him away to the high priest's house.

INFORMATION SPOT

For more information on prophecies fulfilled at Christ's death turn to pages 78-79. To find out more about Peter turn to pages 98-99.

FILE 025/GARDEN OF GETHSEMANE

Gethsemane is located just across the Kidron Valley from Jerusalem. You can still visit it today and see olive trees growing there. Jesus often went to the Garden of Gethsemane. However, on this last occassion it was a place where his spiritual suffering was very great as he anticipated God's wrath being poured out on him. This was the wrath that was meant for God's people. Jesus willingly took it instead to save God's people from their sin.

Jesus is denied by Peter

SCRIPTURE LOCATION: Matthew 26; Luke 22

THEME: Jesus suffers

The band of soldiers led Jesus away to the palace of Caiaphas, the high priest. There he endured a mockery of a trial. Many witnesses told lies. Their statements did not agree. They accused him of blasphemy. They did not believe he was the Son of God. They spat in his face, slapped him and jeered at him.

Peter followed Jesus to the high priest's palace and lingered in the courtyard, warming himself at the fire along with some others.

A young girl who worked as a doorkeeper at the palace recognised Peter.

'This man was with Jesus, too,' she said.

'Woman, I do not know him,' snapped Peter.

He moved out to the porch just as the cock was first crowing.

After a little while another person said, 'Aren't you one of them, too.'

'I am not,' said Peter hotly.

Then someone said, 'This man was with Jesus – he is a Galilean.'

'I don't know what you are talking about,' replied Peter in a panic.

Just then a cock crowed for the second time. Jesus turned round and caught Peter's eye. Peter remembered what Jesus had said, 'Before the cock crows twice you will deny me three times.' How ashamed Peter felt. He went outside and wept bitterly. He had let Jesus down. He had denied him.

INFORMATION SPOT

For more information on the Pharisees turn to pages 44-45; 102-103. To find out more about Peter turn to pages 98-99 as well as the story on pages 60-61.

FILE 026/JESUS KNOWS IT ALL

Jesus knew that Peter would deny him. Turn back to pages 48-49. Peter thought he was strong but Jesus knew better. Jesus knows all about us too.

BIBLE DATA 008

Jesus was persecuted. To be persecuted means to be hurt, ridiculed or even killed for following God's ways. Read 2 Timothy 3:12 and John 15:18. Who also will be persecuted? What are Christians supposed to do when persecuted? Read Matthew 5:44 and Romans 12:14. In Luke 23:34 Jesus does this.

Jesus under arrest

SCRIPTURE LOCATION: Matthew 27;
Mark 15; Luke 23; John 18 and 19
THEME: Jesus suffers

Jesus was tied up again and taken to Pilate the Roman Governor.

'Are you really the King of the Jews?' he asked. 'What have you done?'

'My kingdom is not worldly,' Jesus replied.

'But you are a king?' asked Pilate.

'You can say that I am a king,' stated Jesus. 'The whole purpose of my life is to tell people the truth.'

Pilate went out to the Jewish crowd and said, 'I do not find any fault with this man.'

The people would not agree. 'He is a trouble maker, he stirs up the people, he was always preaching his doctrine throughout the land.'

When Pilate heard that Jesus was from Galilee he passed him to King Herod, who was in Jerusalem at that time. Herod was pleased to see this man about whom he had heard so much. He asked him many questions but Jesus remained silent.

Herod and the soldiers cruelly mocked him, dressed him in a purple robe and sent

him back to Pilate. However, Pilate could still find no fault. 'I have power to release one prisoner during this feast week. I could release Jesus,' he suggested to the crowd.

'No,' they shouted. 'Not this man. Release Barabbas.' Barabbas was a murderer and robber in prison for his crimes.

Pilate appealed to the crowd again, but they shouted out, 'Crucify him! Crucify him!'

Eventually Pilate gave in to their demands. He took some water and washed his hands. 'I am innocent of killing this good man,' he said. He foolishly thought that washing his hands would cleanse the guilt of his part in handing Jesus over to the soldiers.

The soldiers took Jesus and stripped off his clothes and put a royal robe on him. They made a crown of thorns and rammed it on his head. They put a reed in his hand like a sceptre. Then they pretended to bow down to him, making fun of him.

Still Pilate insisted, 'I find no fault in him.'

In the end the wicked men had their way. Jesus was led away to be crucified.

INFORMATION SPOT

For more information on Pilate the Roman Governor turn to pages 100-101.

FILE 027/CRUCIFIXION

Crucifixion was a slow and painful death. It was so degrading and painful that Roman citizens were never crucified themselves. However the sinless son of God was executed alongside criminals.

Jesus on the cross

SCRIPTURE LOCATION: matthew 27;
Luke 23; John 19
THEME: Jesus the Saviour

Jesus was led away to be crucified. He was forced to carry a large wooden cross to Calvary just outside the city wall. Crowds of people followed. Many women wept loudly. His hands and feet were nailed to the cross and he was left hanging there in terrible pain. However, Jesus bore this suffering without complaint. He even prayed to God, 'Father, forgive them for they do not know what they are doing.'

The soldiers took Jesus' garment and cut it into four parts. Each of them took a piece. His coat was made of one piece of material. One of them said, 'Let's cast lots and the winner can take it all.' Even that small detail had been foretold many years before in the book of Psalms.

Jesus' mother Mary stood near the cross, watching. Jesus noticed his mother and his disciple John. Jesus said to his mother, 'Look on John as your son now.' To John he said, 'Treat Mary like your mother.' John looked after Mary from then on.

Two thieves were crucified with Jesus, one on either side. One complained to Jesus, 'If you are Christ, why can't you save yourself and us.' The other one was indignant. 'We deserve this punishment,' he said, 'but this man has done nothing wrong.'

He turned to Jesus and said, 'Remember me when you come into your kingdom.

'Today you shall be with me in heaven,' Jesus assured him.

This man was saved just at the end of his life.

After being on the cross for six hours, Jesus reached the depths of his suffering, 'My God, my God,' he called out, 'why have you left me?' He felt completely alone.

When he called out, 'I am thirsty,' he was given a sponge soaked in vinegar.

After he had drunk some vinegar, he called out, 'It is finished,' then in a loud voice, 'Father into your hands I commend my spirit.'

Then he bowed his head and died. At that moment the curtain in the temple was torn in two from top to bottom, the earth trembled, the rocks split open and some graves were opened. When one soldier saw all this happening he was very afraid. 'Certainly, this man was the Son of God.'

INFORMATION SPOT

For more information on the death of Christ turn to pages 108-109 and pages 78-79.

FILE 028/GOD'S PLAN OF SALVATION

Jesus' suffering and death were part of a wonderful plan of salvation for his people. All sin deserves to be punished. Jesus took the full weight of the just wrath of God on himself so that those who put their trust in him could be saved.

Jesus' burial

SCRIPTURE LOCATION: Matthew 27; Mark 16; Luke 23; John 19

THEME: Jesus triumphs

In the evening a rich man called Joseph from Arimathea went boldly to Pilate to ask if he might have Jesus' body to bury him in his own tomb. His request was granted.

Joseph, helped by Nicodemus, took Jesus' body from the cross, and wrapped it in a linen cloth. They carried the body through a garden and laid it carefully in the tomb, which was a cave. Then they rolled a big stone over the mouth of the cave.

The chief priest and Pharisees remembered that Jesus had said that he would rise from the dead on the third day. They reminded Pilate of this. 'Give orders that the tomb is made very secure until the third day,' they said, 'just in case his disciples come and steal the body and say he is risen.'

'Go,' said Pilate, 'and make it as secure as you can.'

The stone was specially sealed and a guard was set to watch.

Very early in the morning on the first day of the week, Mary Magdalene and two other ladies came to the tomb to anoint Jesus' body with spices. On the way they discussed the problem. 'Who will roll away the stone from the tomb for us?'

When they reached the tomb they were so surprised; the stone had been rolled away already. Mary Magdalene rushed off to find Peter and John. The other two ladies looked inside the tomb and found two angels. 'Do not be afraid,' one said. 'I know you are looking for Jesus. Do not look for him here. He is risen from the dead.'

INFORMATION SPOT

For more information on the resurrection turn to pages 110-111. To find out more about Pilate turn to pages 100-101.

FILE 29/BURIAL

In New Testament times wealthy people were buried in chambers cut into the soft limestone rock of Palestine. The tomb was then sealed with a large round stone slab across the entrance. Matthew 27:57-60 gives a similar description of Jesus' tomb.

FILE 030/EYE WITNESSES

When the ladies looked in they saw the angels and the neatly folded clothes. It is interesting to read precise details like this in the Bible. It is what eye witnesses remembered seeing. The authorities later falsely accused the disciples of stealing Jesus' body - but a thief wouldn't stop and fold clothes - he would run. This false story was a lie created by the Pharisees and the guards to cover the truth.

The resurrection

SCRIPTURE LOCATION: John 20 and 21

THEME: Jesus triumphs

The first person to see the risen Lord Jesus was Mary Magdalene. She came back to the garden, weeping because she thought Jesus' body had been stolen. A man came to speak to her. 'Why are you crying?' he asked. 'Who are you looking for?'

She thought this man was the gardener. She said, 'Sir, if you have taken him away, please tell me where you have laid his body.'

The man said to her, 'Mary.'

She then realised that the man was the risen Lord Jesus.

'Master!' she cried out.

Jesus then gave her instructions to go to the disciples and to tell them that he was returning to his Father and their Father, to his God and their God. Mary ran with the good news to the disciples.

'I have seen the Lord,' she exclaimed. Then she told the disciples all that Jesus had told her.

In the evening the frightened disciples were hiding in a locked room. There was no other way in but just then Jesus appeared and stood among them. 'Peace be with you,' he said. He showed them his hands and his side, which had been pierced.

The disciples were glad when they saw the Lord. This changed every thing.

But one disciple, Thomas was not there. When he was told the news he couldn't believe it. 'Unless I see the print of the nails and put my hand into them and into his side, I will not believe,' he said to them.

Eight days later Jesus again appeared to the disciples. This time Thomas was there too. Jesus said to Thomas, 'Reach your finger here to my hands, put your hand in my side. Do not doubt, but believe.'

Thomas did believe then. 'My Lord and my God!' he exclaimed.

Later seven disciples went fishing on the Sea of Galilee. They fished all night but caught nothing. As they came back to the shore they noticed a man standing there.

'Have you anything to eat?' the man asked. 'No,' they replied.

'Put your net down again,' he told them.

They did as he said and the catch was so large, 153 fish.

John realised that the man on the beach was Jesus. 'It is the Lord,' he gasped.

Peter jumped into the sea to rush ashore ahead of the boat. The others followed dragging the net of fish. When they all reached the shore there was a fire lit with fish already cooking and bread too. Jesus invited them to bring some of the fish that they had caught. 'Come and have something to eat,' he said.

They all knew that this was Jesus.

INFORMATION SPOT

For more information on the resurrection turn to pages 110-111.

FILE 031/RESURRECTION

There is proof for the resurrection. Jesus appeared after his death to Mary Magdalene and the other women; Peter; eleven disciples; two on Emmaus road; 500 people; James and the apostles.

SCRIPTURE LOCATION: Luke 24

The road to Emmaus

THEME: Jesus teaches and preaches

Cleopas and a friend were walking from Jerusalem to Emmaus, about seven miles away. They discussed the amazing things that had happened in Jerusalem in the past few days.

Jesus came along beside them and walked with them, but they did not recognize him.

'What have you been speaking about?' Jesus asked.

'Don't you know what has been happening in Jerusalem these past few days?' demanded Cleopas.

'What things?' asked Jesus.

'The things that happened to Jesus,' answered Cleopas. 'The chief priests and rulers condemned him to death and crucified him. We had hoped that he would be the Saviour of our people. Three days have passed since his death. Some women went early to his tomb but they found it empty. Angels told them he was alive. Some of our friends went to the tomb but they did not see Jesus.'

Jesus gently rebuked them. 'You are so slow to believe what has been told you by the prophets. Christ had to suffer all these things before he entered glory.'

Jesus explained to them all the Old Testament scriptures, which referred to himself. When they reached Emmaus, Jesus seemed to intend carrying on further. They begged him, 'Please stay with us, it is late now.'

Jesus went into the house with them and sat down for supper. He took the bread, blessed it and broke off a piece for each of them. Only then did they recognise the risen Lord Jesus. Immediately he vanished from their sight.

'That explains how we felt as he spoke to us on the road,' they said to each other.

They rushed back to Jerusalem to share their wonderful news with the eleven disciples and others. 'The Lord really has risen,' they said.

INFORMATION SPOT

For more information on Jesus and the Bible turn to pages 70-71 and pages 20-21. To find out the location of Emmaus on the map turn to pages 68-69.

FILE 032/OLD TESTAMENT PROPHECY

The Old Testament tells us a lot about Christ. Psalm 22 speaks of his suffering and pain. Isaiah 53 tells of the man of sorrows, acquainted with bitter grief. Zechariah points to the death of the Messiah in Jerusalem, even saying he would ride in on a young donkey. Many details foretold in the Old Testament came to pass that week in Jerusalem.

The ascension

SCRIPTURE LOCATION: Luke 24; Acts 1

THEME: Jesus is worshipped

Jesus and his disciples went out to the Mount of Olives near Bethany.

Jesus spoke to his disciples about the future and said to them, 'I will send the Holy Spirit to help you and you will be my witnesses in Jerusalem, and Judea and Samaria, right to the furthest corner of the earth.'

As he said these words he lifted up his hands and blessed them. His body was then lifted up from the ground and soon a cloud hid him from their sight. The disciples stood gazing up into the heavens where Jesus went. Then two angels in white stood beside them. 'Why are you standing here, looking up to heaven?' they asked. 'Jesus who was taken up to heaven will one day return in the same way.'

This filled the disciples with joy. They worshipped God and went back to Jerusalem to start preaching the good news of the Word of God.

Jesus is alive today. He is in heaven but also with his people here. He cares for us and is continually praying to God the Father for his people. Jesus will return to the world again, we are told that he will return with a shout, with the voice of an archangel and with the trumpet of God. Christians who have died will rise from the grave (just as Christ did). Those Christians who are still alive will meet the Lord in the air. We do not know when this will happen. It is all in God's hands.

Jesus did many things, which are not written in the Bible. But the details we have are written so that we might believe in him and have him as our Saviour and friend.

INFORMATION SPOT

For more information on Jesus the Saviour turn to pages 92-93 and pages 108-111.

FILE 033/JESUS TODAY

Jesus is in heaven seated at the right hand of God. Jesus is also in the hearts of his people. Where two or three are gathered in his name, Jesus is there with them.

BIBLE DATA 009

Read John 21:25. What does the gospel writer tell us here about all the things that Jesus did?

Today and the future

SCRIPTURE LOCATION: Matthew 6, 16; Acts 2; Hebrews 7; James 5

THEME: Jesus will be worshipped

Jesus is alive

He is now exalted again and in heaven. What is he doing today? Read Hebrews 7:25 Jesus is continually praying for his people. He is our great High Priest.

Jesus is with his people

Jesus cares for us in many ways. When we are together to worship God, he is there. We do not see him with our eyes, but his presence is real and he blesses and helps us.

Jesus is building his church

The church is not a building but is the group of believing people who meet together to worship God. The Lord is adding daily to the church those whom he has saved. Matthew 16:18; Acts 2:47.

Jesus is preparing his people for heaven

He is making his people more like himself. He is keeping everything in the world in existence. In him we live and move and have our being.

Jesus has promised to return to this world again

He will come suddenly, when we do not expect it – like a thief in the night. He will come down from heaven with a shout, with the voice of an archangel and with the trumpet of God. No one will miss this great event. Every knee will bow to him. Jesus will judge the world. Those who believed in him will be blessed. They will be raised with new bodies. Christ, the Judge, will declare them free from all guilt. They will be taken to heaven to be forever with the Lord.

INFORMATION SPOT

For more information on the relationship between Jesus and us, as human beings, his creation and his people turn to pages 74-75; 86-87 and 92-93.

FILE 034/JESUS IN THE FUTURE

Jesus is coming back to earth for a second time. When he came the first time he came as a vulnerable baby, but he will return as a victorious King. 'Be patient therefore, brothers, until the coming of the Lord ... Establish your hearts, for the coming of the Lord is at hand,' James 5:7.

BIBLE DATA 010

What does the Bible tell us about the future? Read Matthew 6:27-34 and Matthew 28:20 to find out.

21.

19.

16.

18.

4. .8
7.   .9
3.   17.
25. 13.   .11
23.   24.
6.   5.
2. 22.   .20
1.
14.

12.

10.

15.

Bible times map

PURPOSE: Look at the names below. The numbers will help you work out where each place is located on the map.

1. Bethlehem
2. Jerusalem
3. Nazareth
4. Capernaum
5. Jericho
6. Emmaus
7. Cana
8. Bethsaida
9. Sea of Galilee
10. Nile
11. Jordan River
12. Mediterranean Sea
13. Samaria
14. Judea
15. Egypt
16. Tyre

17. Gadera
18. Caesarea Philippi
19. Sidon
20. Dead Sea
21. Cyprus
22. Bethany
23. Joppa
24. Arimathea
25. Caesarea

Jesus and the Bible

SCRIPTURE LOCATION: Matthew 4, 12, 27

LINK BACK: Pages 20-21; 56-57

Temptation in the desert

Jesus knew the scriptures and quoted from them throughout his life and ministry. It was an important part of Jesus' own defence against the Devil at the temptation in the wilderness. During the temptation he quoted from Deuteronomy.

Warnings from Jonah and the Queen of Sheba

Pharisees and teachers of the law demanded to see a miraculous sign from Jesus.

'You have been given the sign from the prophet Jonah,' Jesus replied. 'Just as Jonah was three days and three nights in the stomach of a huge fish, so the Son of Man (Jesus) will be three days and three nights in the grave. The men of Nineveh repented when Jonah preached. One greater than Jonah is here now. The Queen of Sheba came a great distance to hear Solomon's wisdom. Now one greater than Solomon is here.' Jesus used the Bible stories found in the book of Jonah and 1 Kings 10.

Preaching in the synagogue

One day Jesus went to his home town Nazareth and, as usual, went to the service at the synagogue on the Sabbath day. He stood up and read from Isaiah. 'The Spirit of the Lord is upon me because he has anointed me to preach good news to the poor. He has sent me to proclaim freedom for the prisoners, the recovery of sight for the blind, to release the oppressed, to proclaim the year of the Lord's favour,' Isaiah 61:1-5.

When he began to preach he explained that Isaiah's prophetic words were fulfilled in their hearing that day. The Lord Jesus himself was the one spoken about. His hearers were amazed at his gracious words.

On the Cross

When Jesus was suffering on the cross he quoted from Psalm 22. The first verse of this psalm is exactly what Jesus said on the cross, 'My God, my God, why have you forsaken me?'

Things others said about Jesus

SCRIPTURE LOCATION: 1 Peter 2; Colossians 1; John 1; Revelation 5, 19

LINK BACK: Pages 16-17; 36-37

God the Father

God spoke from heaven at the time that Jesus was baptised and called him, 'My beloved Son in whom I am well pleased,' Matthew 3:17. In Matthew 17:5 we read how God used these same words when Jesus was transfigured on the mountain with Moses and Elijah. Jesus is the Son of God.

John the Baptist

John pointed the people to Jesus. 'Behold the Lamb of God,' he said, 'who takes away the sin of the world,' John 1:29. In Old Testament times a lamb was killed as a sacrifice for sins. Jesus was the sacrifice for the sins of his people. We can read about this in the following verse from the Bible: 'Christ was offered once to bear the sins of many,' Hebrews 9:28. He is the only one who has the power to cleanse us from our sin.

The Apostle Paul

Paul wrote many letters to churches and individuals. In one of his letters to Timothy (2 Timothy 4:1) he speaks of Jesus as the Judge of the living and the dead. Those who believe in Christ are declared righteous because of what he has done. Those who do not believe are condemned by him. In the letter to the church at Colosse Paul speaks of Jesus as the Head of the Church. He controls every part of it and gives it life and direction.

The Apostle Peter

Peter in his letters to Christians (1 Peter 2:7) tells of Jesus as the Chief Cornerstone. In a building the chief cornerstone would keep the wall safe and secure. Jesus is the safety and security for his people. More information about cornerstones is on page 91.

The Apostle John

In Revelation 5:5-6 John depicts Jesus as the Lion of the tribe of Judah – showing his strength and power. He also shows him to be a Lamb – standing but as though it had been slain. Jesus died for sinners but is alive again. In Revelation 19:16 John also called Jesus the King of Kings and Lord of Lords.

In the Gospel of John the apostle says of the Lord Jesus, 'In the beginning was the Word, and the Word was with God, and the Word was God. He was in the beginning with God. All things were made through him, and without him was not anything made that was made.' There is no one higher or more powerful or more glorious than Jesus Christ.

INFORMATION SPOT

For more information about what Jesus was called, turn to pages 8-9; 18-19 and 36-37. To find out more about John the Baptist turn to pages 96-97 and Peter turn to pages 98-99.

Jesus and prayer

SCRIPTURE LOCATION: Matthew 6; John 17; Acts 1

LINK BACK: Pages 50-51; 56-57

When did Jesus pray?

Jesus prayed continually. He communicated regularly with his father and at special times. Those special times were:

In the morning – long before daybreak (Mark 1:35).

All night (Luke 6:12).

In the evening (Matthew 14:23).

Before he had important work to do (Matthew 26:36).

Where did Jesus pray?

He would have prayed in many different places but here are some of the specific places mentioned in the Bible:

A mountain (Matthew 14:23).

The Garden of Gethsemane (Matthew 26:36).

A Solitary place (Mark 1:35).

The Wilderness (Luke 5:16).

The Lord's Prayer

Jesus knew how important prayer was. So he taught his disciples how to pray. Here is what he taught his disciples to pray when they asked him to teach them.

'Our Father in heaven, hallowed be your name. Your kingdom come. Your will be done on earth as it is in heaven. Give us this day our daily bread. And forgive us our debts, As we forgive our debtors. And do not lead us into temptation, But deliver us from the evil one. For yours is the kingdom and the power and the glory forever. Amen.'

Who did he pray for?

In John 17 we have a wonderful example of Jesus praying to the Father.

He prays for himself as he contemplates his approaching death.

He prays too for his disciples, that they would be united to God and to each other. He prayed that they would be kept from the evil one.

Jesus then prayed for all believers in times to come – that they would all be one and behold his glory.

Jesus gave thanks for food at the outside picnic for 5,000 people and at the last supper with his disciples.

On the cross Jesus prayed for those who were cruelly killing him. 'Father, forgive them,' he prayed, 'for they do not know what they are doing.'

Devote yourself to prayer

The way Jesus prayed is a good example for us. There are other good examples of prayer in the Bible. In Acts 1:12-14 we read that after the death and resurrection of Jesus Christ the disciples devoted themselves to prayer - together with the women and Mary the mother of Jesus and his brothers.

Prophecies fulfilled at Birth

SCRIPTURE LOCATION: Micah 5; Isaiah 7, 9; Genesis 3, 12, 17; Numbers 24

LINK BACK: Pages 8-15

Prophecies

In the Old Testament, God told his people that he would send the Saviour. This promised One was known as the Messiah or the Christ. Jesus fulfilled all these prophecies.

Christ would be born in Bethlehem (Micah 5:2)

'But you Bethlehem Ephrathah, though you are little among the thousands of Judah, yet out of you shall come forth to me, the One to be ruler in Israel, whose goings forth are from of old, from everlasting.' The Prophet Micah pinpointed the exact place of Christ's birth. Bethlehem Ephratha was a small town south of Jerusalem. (Ephrathah distinguishes the town from another Bethlehem - in Galilee).

Christ would be born of a virgin (Isaiah 7:14)

'The Lord himself will give you a sign, behold, the virgin shall conceive and bear a Son, and shall call his name Immanuel.' (God with us). Mary knew that she had no relationship with a man. The angel told her that the child was conceived by the power of God, the Holy Spirit. He was truly human and truly divine.

Some of Christ's ancestors are referred to

Eve (Genesis 3:15) - Christ, the seed of the woman (Eve) would crush the head of the serpent. The serpent is the devil. When Jesus died on the cross the Devil was crushed and finally defeated.

Abraham (Genesis 12:3) - God said to him - 'in you all the families of the earth shall be blessed.' Paul in the letter to the Galatians said that this was 'the gospel to Abraham beforehand.' All nations are blessed through Jesus, a descendant of Abraham, because he died to purchase salvation for people from every nation, tribe and language.

Isaac (Genesis 17:19) - God said to Abraham, 'Sarah shall bear you a son and you shall call his name Isaac: I will establish my covenant with him, for an everlasting covenant.' When Jesus was born he was the fulfilment of this covenant. Everlasting life came to God's people through Jesus Christ.

Jacob (Numbers 24:17) - 'A star shall come out of Jacob: a sceptre will rise out of Israel.' The star refers to Jesus as the Light of the World. The sceptre points to the fact that he is King of Kings. Jesus is a light to show us our sin and need of salvation. He is a King because all authority in heaven and on earth is his. (Matthew 28:18)

Judah (Genesis 49:10) - 'The sceptre shall not depart from Judah until Shiloh comes.' Judah was the tribe that Jesus was born into. Shiloh referred to the Messiah. Christ is called the Lion of the tribe of Judah in the book of Revelation.

David (Isaiah 9:7) - 'For unto us a child is born, unto us a son is given ... He will reign upon the throne of David and over his kingdom to order it and establish it with judgement and justice.' King David was an ancestor of Jesus. Jesus is the King of Kings. David was Israel's king but he was only a man and a sinner. Jesus would be greater than David in every way. His kingdom would last for ever.

BIBLE DATA 011

In which of the places in Isaiah 9:1-2 did Jesus perform many miracles? Where was he baptised? What two words are mentioned in Isaiah 9:2 and John 8:12. Who do these verses speak about?

Prophecies fulfilled at Death

SCRIPTURE LOCATION: Isaiah 53; Psalm 22, 34, 69; John 19

LINK BACK: Pages 52-59

The Prophet Isaiah foretold many of the events around the death of the Lord Jesus Christ. You can read Isaiah's prophecies in the Old Testament in the Book of Isaiah.

Isaiah 53:3 – 'He was despised and rejected by men, a man of sorrows and acquainted with grief.' Jesus was hated and rejected and suffered abuse and grief.

Isaiah 53:5 – 'He was wounded for our transgressions; he was bruised for our iniquities.' Here we see how Christ suffered in our place – not for his sins (for he had none) but for ours.

Isaiah 53:7 – 'As a sheep before her shearers is silent, so he opened not his mouth.' Jesus was completely submissive to those who were against him.

Isaiah 53:9 – 'He was assigned a grave with the wicked – but was with the rich at his death.' Jesus was crucified with two criminals but he was not buried with them as would have been expected. Joseph of Arimathea, a rich man, asked to be allowed to take Jesus' body and bury it in his own grave.

Isaiah 53:12 – 'He was numbered with the transgressors.' This is another verse that prophesied that Jesus was to be crucified between two criminals.

Psalm 22:10 – David, in the book of Psalms, foretells some details which happened when Jesus died. 'They divide my garments amongst themselves, and for my clothing they cast lots.'

John 19:23-24 – If you look at these verses you will read how the soldiers who crucified Jesus did indeed take his garment and divide it. His tunic was made of one piece of cloth, so rather than tear it, they cast lots and the winner took the whole thing.

Psalm 34:20 – This psalm foretells that not one of Jesus' bones would be broken. The two men who were crucified with Jesus had their legs broken but Jesus' legs were not broken.

Psalm 69:21 – When Jesus was on the cross he uttered the words, 'I am thirsty' so that the scripture in Psalm 69 would be fulfilled.

Psalm 22:16 – 'They pierced my hands and feet,' says David in this psalm. That is exactly what happened to Jesus as he was crucified.

BIBLE DATA 012

Read Psalm 22:1. Now read Mark 15:34. Can you see any similarities?

Miracles of healing

SCRIPTURE LOCATION: Mark 2, 7, 10; Luke 4, 6, 13, 17

LINK BACK: Pages 38-39

Jesus the healer

Jesus healed many people from many different diseases. The following are just a few of the amazing things he did for others:

The blind were made to see (Mark 10)

Bartimaeus was a blind beggar until Jesus met him on the road to Jericho. 'Jesus, Son of David, have mercy on me,' he said. 'What do you want?' Jesus asked. 'To receive my sight,' he replied. 'Your faith has made you well,' said Jesus. At once he could see.

The dumb were able to speak and the deaf able to hear (Mark 7)

A man was brought to Jesus because he was deaf and dumb. Jesus put his fingers in his ears and touched his tongue with saliva. He looked to heaven and said, 'Be opened.' Immediately his ears could hear and his tongue was able to speak plainly.

The lepers were cleansed (Luke 17)

Leprosy was an infectious disease. If you suffered from it you had to leave your family and live as an outcast. Jesus met ten lepers one day. They pleaded for help and Jesus cleansed them. They all went to the priest to be pronounced clean and able to go home. Only one came back to Jesus to say thank you.

The paralysed were able to walk (Mark 2)

In Capernaum there was a man who could not walk. Four friends took him to Jesus on a mat. They had to climb up to a roof. In Bible times a roof was flat and you could gain access to it by a flight of steps at the side of the house. Once on the roof they made a large hole and lowered the man down in front of Jesus. Jesus forgave his sins and said - 'Get up, take your bed and walk.' The man got up at once and walked home.

The sick were cured (Luke 4)

One Sabbath day Jesus went from the synagogue to Peter's house. Peter's mother-in-law was very sick with a fever. Jesus was asked to help. He stood over her and rebuked her fever and it left her. She was well enough to help to serve the meal.

The crippled were made straight (Luke 13)

A woman had suffered for eighteen years with a deformed back. She was bent double. She could not stand straight. Jesus met her on Sabbath in the synagogue. He spoke to her, put his hands on her and immediately she could stand up straight.

The dead were raised to life (Luke 7)

As well as Jairus' daughter, Jesus also raised the widow of Nain's son. During the funeral procession Jesus touched the coffin and the young man was restored to his mother.

The withered hand was restored (Luke 6)

The man's withered hand hung uselessly at his side. 'Stretch out your hand,' said Jesus. He was able to do that. Jesus had healed him.

INFORMATION SPOT

For more information about healing read the story about the woman who bled for twelve years on pages 30-31. This story can also be read in the gospel of Mark 5:21-34.

Other miracles

SCRIPTURE LOCATION: Matthew 15, 17; Mark 4, 6; Luke 5
LINK BACK: Pages 60-61

The Creator of all things

The Lord Jesus Christ, the Son of God, did many amazing miracles. He was the Creator of all things and so had power over all his creation.

He had power over the sea

Once when he and the disciples were caught in a big storm of the Sea of Galilee, he spoke to the wind and waves and said, 'Peace, be still.' Immediately there was calm.

He had power to walk on top of the water, out over the sea to the boat where his disciples were sailing. They were frightened at first – then Peter wanted to walk out to meet Jesus. When he took his eyes off Jesus and looked at the waves, he began to sink but Jesus caught him.

He had power over nature

The temple authorities required every man to pay for the upkeep of the temple. 'Does your master pay the temple tax?' they asked Peter. 'O, yes,' he replied.

Jesus explained to Peter that as he was the Son of God, he ought to be freed from this tax: but to avoid giving offence he would pay.

'Go to the sea and throw a hook into the sea. Take the first fish that comes up. You will find a piece of money in its mouth. Pay the tax for you and me with that coin.'

He had the power to provide

On one occasion Jesus fed a huge crowd of people starting with a very small amount of food. He blessed the food, broke it up and the food was multiplied to satisfy everyone. 5,000 men plus women and children were fed with five little loaves and two small fish and twelve baskets of fragments were gathered up.

On another occassion 4,000 men, women and children were fed with just seven loaves and a few fish and on that occassion seven baskets of left-overs were gathered up.

Through Jesus' power over nature and living things, his disciples were able to catch a huge haul of fish - a grand total of 153!

INFORMATION SPOT

For more information about miracles and Jesus' power over nature read the story on pages 28-29.

BIBLE DATA 013

Jesus performed many great miracles. He also rose from the dead. Read Luke 24: 1-12. In 1 Corinthians 1:18 we are told something amazing about God's power. What is this?

Other parables

SCRIPTURE LOCATION: Matthew 7, 13, 25; Luke 15, 16, 18

LINK BACK: Pages 32-33; 38-39; 42-43

Jesus used many stories to teach about God, his word and salvation. Here are a few for you to read up about:

The wise and foolish builder (Matthew 7:24-27)
This parable is about the importance of obeying God's word and having Jesus as the foundation of our life.

Weeds in the corn field (Matthew 13:24-30)
Jesus teaches us here about the Judgement day. On that day there will be a difference between those who love the Lord Jesus and those who do not. Those who love the Lord will go to heaven to be with him. Those who don't love God will be lost and rejected.

Mustard seed, Hidden treasure, Costly pearl (Matthew 13:31-46)
Jesus uses several stories here to show us that the work of God in a person's heart may start in a small and insignificant way but it is of great importance.

Lost sheep; Lost coin (Luke 15:3-10)

God goes to great trouble to save sinners. He loves sinners so much that he sent his Son to die for them. Those who believe in him have eternal life.

Wise and foolish bridesmaids (Matthew 25:1-13)

In this story Jesus teaches us about the importance of being ready to meet with God.

Pharisee and tax collector (Luke 18:9-14)

Jesus teaches us about the need to realise that we are sinners and need a saviour.

Rich man and Lazarus (Luke 16:19-31)

Here we learn about the importance of believing the Bible and trusting in Christ. After death it is too late.

Persistent widow (Luke 18:1-8)

This parable teaches us that it is good to keep on praying to God and not to give up.

Other things that Jesus taught

SCRIPTURE LOCATION: Matthew 7, 18, Luke 11; John 3, 6, 14; 1 John

LINK BACK: Pages 18-19; 42-43; 74-75

Preaching

To preach means to announce a message. It also means to announce good news. Jesus preached and people were often amazed at the strength of his words. 'He speaks as though he has authority.' Jesus was in charge. You could tell by the words he spoke.

Jesus taught us what God is like

Jesus said that God is like a father who cares for his child. If a child asks his father for some bread he will not give him a stone instead.

God listens to our prayers and wants to help us just as a loving father wants to help his child. In 1 John 4:16 it says that 'God is love.' In John 3:16 we are told how that is true, 'For God so loved the world that he gave his only son that whoever believes in him should not perish but have eternal life.'

Jesus taught us how to get to heaven

Jesus taught that there is only one way to heaven. He said, 'I am the way the truth and the life. No one can get to God the Father except by me.'

Jesus taught us how to live and love others

Jesus used a child to illustrate how people should behave. 'The one who is as humble as this little child is the greatest in the kingdom of heaven,' Jesus explained. Jesus taught that we should forgive people and treat others as we would like to be treated. All people are our neighbours and we should show mercy to them.

Jesus taught us how to be happy

The first and most important way to be truly happy is to trust in Jesus Christ. It is only through him that we can be saved from the punishment our sins deserve and it is only through him that we can be truly satisfied with life. Jesus used a loaf of bread as an illustration to show us this. He said, 'I am the bread of life. No one who comes to me will ever be hungry and the one who believes in me will never thirst.' Jesus is the only one who can satisfy the longings we have in our souls.

INFORMATION SPOT

To find out more about heaven and who is there turn to pages 64-65.

BIBLE DATA 014

What different sorts of people did Jesus speak to? Read Matthew 4:18-22; 8:18-22; 9:9-12; 11:20-24; 12:1-8; 15:21-28; 19:13-15; Luke 7:36-50; 19:1-10; John 3:1-21.

Names of Jesus

Jesus uses picture language

Jesus taught a lot about himself by using picture language to describe himself or his work. He used pictures such as bread and light and door - the words 'I AM' are used alongside many of these. This is because these two little words have great significance.

I Am Who I Am

When Moses met with God in the wilderness by the burning bush God told him to tell Pharaoh to let the Israelite people go. But Moses was concerned that the Israelite people might not believe him when he said to them that the God of their fathers had sent him. 'Who shall I say has sent me?' Moses asked. God then said, 'I AM WHO I AM' tell them that 'I AM' has sent you.'

The name 'I AM' then has a great significance throughout the Bible and when Jesus uses it in the New Testament it was meant to jog people's memories. This name had such great significance that it annoyed the Pharisees immensely when Jesus used it. They knew that Jesus was claiming to be God. Jesus' claim was true.

The following names that Jesus gives to himself make use of the words I AM. Each of these names has its own special meaning.

I am the bread of life:

Jesus gives feeding and nourishment to the soul.

I am the light of the world:

Jesus gives guidance and leading and clears away the darkness of evil.

I am the door:

Only through Jesus do we have access to God the Father.

I am the good shepherd:

Jesus loves and cares for those who follow him and provides for their needs.

I am the resurrection and the life:

Jesus has power over life and death. He rose from the dead. He will raise the dead.

I am the way, the truth and the life:

No one comes to God, except through Jesus.

I am the true vine you are the branches:

We depend on Jesus for life.

Other important names of Jesus

The Word

Jesus is called the Word. He existed when the world began. He was God and was with God. Read John 1:1 and John 1:14. These verses show you where in the Bible Jesus was referred to as the Word.

Immanuel

This means 'God with us'. He became a man and lived in this world, just like us. He was both God and man. Read Isaiah 7:14 and Matthew 1:23. These verses show you where in the Bible Jesus was referred to as Immanuel.

Saviour

Jesus means Saviour. He is the one who saves his people from their sins. The name Saviour is mentioned a lot in the Bible. Read Psalm 17:7; Luke 1:47 and John 4:42 to find out a bit more about this.

Lamb of God

His life was given as a sacrifice to satisfy God's just demands to punish sin. The Jews would sacrifice a lamb in the temple. Lambs were sacrificed by the Israelites the night before they left Egypt. Jesus' parents sacrificed a pair of turtle doves or two young

pigeons on Jesus' first visit to the temple. However we no longer have to go through with these rituals anymore. Jesus' death did away with the need for those sacrifices.

Holy One of God

Jesus was completely sinless in his life and nature. We can sin in so many ways - we can sin in our actions by doing something wrong or selfish. We can sin by not doing something that we should have done. We can also sin by thinking wrong thoughts and by saying words that displease God. Jesus did none of this. It is because of his sinless nature that he was the perfect sacrifice for sin.

Chief Cornerstone

Jesus is the sure foundation for life. When a builder is constructing a house he must have a strong foundation to build the house upon. Builders in Bible times would have referred to a cornerstone as being a very important part of the building. Jesus should be the most important person in our lives.

King of Kings, Lord of Lords

Jesus is the almighty God – greater than any king. Every knee will bow before him. Everyone will realise who he is and that he is Lord of all.

Jesus the Saviour

SCRIPTURE LOCATION: Acts 16

LINK BACK: Pages 9; 23; 65

Who will rescue us?

A saviour is someone who rescues another person from danger. Jesus' name means Saviour. Jesus' name was chosen by God. Mary and Joseph were told by God to call the baby Jesus for he would save his people from their sins. It was through Jesus' death on the cross and his resurrection that his people are saved from sin.

Why do people need to be saved?

We are sinners. Sin is not just a sickness, it is part of us. It is destructive and evil. People are made up of three parts, body, mind and soul. Our soul is the part of us that loves or doesn't love God. It is our soul that will go on living after we die. If we have been saved by Jesus our soul will go to heaven. If we have not accepted the gift of salvation from Christ our soul will be sent to Hell - a place of tears, sin and anger.

How are we saved?

You should read the story of the Philippian Jailor in Acts 16:16-34. He asked Paul how he could be saved. Paul replied, 'Believe in the Lord Jesus Christ and you will be saved, you and your household.'

Who is the Saviour?

Jesus Christ is the Saviour of the world but it was God the Father who sent Jesus into the world to save his people from their sins. Salvation is given to us because of Christ's death on the cross and because God sent his one and only son to do this.

What happens after salvation?

God makes our souls alive instead of dead. Our souls are dead until Jesus saves us and gives us spiritual life. God now changes us to love him and he gives us a work to do - to praise him, please him and to enjoy him for ever. We don't have to be afraid of an angry God because Jesus' death on the cross has taken God's anger away from us.

What do we do?

Salvation is God's work and his gift. What you do is to receive it when it is offered to you. When we are sinners we do not love God and we do not want anything from him. But when God changes us he changes our heart and he even helps us to turn to him and ask for help and salvation. So God gives us salvation and he gives us the ability to receive the gift too. It's all God's work.

BIBLE DATA 015

Read these verses and answer the questions:

1 John 4:14. Who sent Jesus as the Saviour?

Romans 10:13: Who can obtain salvation?

Acts 4:10-12: Where do we find salvation?

Isaiah 55:1; Romans 6:23: Will it cost us anything?

Revelation 5:9:What did salvation cost Christ?

Mary the mother of Jesus

SCRIPTURE LOCATION: Matthew 1; Luke 1, 2; John 19; Acts 1

LINK BACK: Pages 8-17; 24-25; 57

Mary's home

Mary lived in Nazareth. Joseph, her fiancé was a carpenter there. Though Mary was the mother of Jesus Joseph was not his father - God was his father.

Mary's character

We can learn a lot about Mary's character from the way she reacted to the angel's news. She believed in God and trusted him greatly. Instead of being upset and frightened we read that Mary was full of joy when she realised that the baby she would give birth to would be the special one that God had promised, the Messiah. Mary was also a thoughtful person. When the shepherds came to visit the baby Jesus, Mary treasured these things and kept them in her heart. After Mary and Joseph found the twelve year old Jesus speaking to the temple teachers about God, Mary treasured all these things in her heart.

Mary at the crucifixion

At the crucifixion Jesus told his disciple John to look after Mary and then later after Christ's resurrection Mary is found praying with the disciples, some other women and Christ's brothers.

What does Jesus want us to learn?

Mary's words, 'I am the Lord's Servant', should teach us that God should be first in our lives. Mary was God's servant. This means that her son was more important than she was. At the wedding in Cana Mary told Jesus that the host had run out of wine. But Jesus told her that his time had not yet come. Jesus is always in control. He didn't need his mother to tell him what to do.

Mary's Son

Though Mary was a godly woman, it is her son, Jesus Christ, who has power and authority over all creation. It is to her son, Jesus Christ, that we can go to directly with our prayers and requests, with our hopes and fears and most importantly with our love, in the same way that Mary did. She was a sinner just like us.

FILE 035/WOMEN IN JESUS' FAMILY

Mary is one of five women mentioned in Jesus' family tree in Matthew 1 as are other women: Tamar, Rahab, Ruth and Bathsheba (Uriah's wife and Solomon's mother).

BIBLE DATA 016

For information about Jesus' family tree read Matthew 1; Luke 3 and Romans 1:3. Now read 1 Timothy 6:15 and 2 Timothy 2:8. There are two kings mentioned in these verses who are they? What is the difference between them?

John the Baptist

SCRIPTURE LOCATION: Matthew 3, 14; Mark 1; Luke 1, 7

LINK BACK: Pages 8-9; 18-19; 72

John the Baptist's birth foretold

John the Baptist was a relative of Jesus. His parents were Zechariah and Elizabeth. Before his birth, his father, Zechariah was burning incense in the temple. An angel appeared and told him that he and his wife Elizabeth would have a son and he was to be named John. Zechariah asked the angel how he could be sure of this.

The angel replied, 'I am Gabriel. I stand in the presence of God, and I have been sent to speak to you and to tell you this good news. And now you will not be able to speak until the day this happens, because you did not believe my words.'

So when Zechariah came out of the temple he could not speak a word. Everyone knew something must have happened as he signalled that he had seen a vision.

Elizabeth speaks up

Some months later Elizabeth gave birth and the family gathered for the special ceremony. Some thought that the child would be named after his father but Elizabeth said, 'No! He is to be called John.' Everyone was surprised. No one in their family had that name.

Zechariah asked for a writing tablet and wrote, 'His name is John.' Immediately he was able to speak once again and he began praising God.

John's ministry

John grew up and told people to stop sinning and return to God. He pointed people towards Jesus. He lived a very basic life eating locusts and wild honey and wearing clothes made from camel's hair. Jesus respected John the Baptist and said, 'Among those born of women there has not risen anyone greater than John the Baptist.'

John was put in prison by King Herod. While in prison he told his disciples to ask Jesus if he was the promised Messiah. Jesus replied, 'Tell him what you hear and see: the blind receive their sight, the lame walk, lepers are cleansed, the deaf hear, the dead are raised to life and the good news is preached to the poor.'

The death of John the Baptist

Herodias' daughter danced for Herod and his guests. Herod rashly promised to give her anything she wanted - even up to half of his kingdom. The young girl went to her mother for advice. The woman instructed her to ask for the head of John the Baptist. When Herod heard this he was distressed but didn't want to appear foolish in front of his guests so he ordered that her request be granted.

What Jesus wants us to learn from the life of John the Baptist

We should learn to be humble and that we should seek to make Jesus great. John the Baptist said about Jesus, ' He must become greater, I must become less,' John 3:30.

BIBLE DATA 017

Read John 1:19-23. How does this show John the Baptist's humility? Read Isaiah 40:3. Does this verse remind you of another verse from the Bible?

Peter the Apostle

SCRIPTURE LOCATION: Matthew 4, 10, 16, 26; Mark 16; Luke 22, 24; John 21

LINK BACK: Pages 48-53; 59; 61; 72

Fishers of men

Peter and his brother Andrew met Jesus when they were fishing. Jesus said, 'Come, follow me and I will make you fishers of men.' They left and followed him at once.

What Peter said and saw

Once Jesus asked Peter, 'Who do you say that I am?' Peter replied, 'You are the Christ the Son of the living God.' That was a wonderful thing for Peter to realise. Jesus explained to his disciples that he would have to be killed and on the third day be raised to life. Peter said. 'Never Lord! This shall never happen to you!'

Jesus then turned and addressed Peter, 'Get behind me Satan!'

Jesus was to save people from their sins and the only way this was possible was through his death on the cross. It was wrong of Peter to disagree with the Lord.

Peter saw many wonderful things. He saw people raised from the dead. He saw Jesus walk on water and calm the seas. He was with him at the transfiguration. He witnessed healings and other miracles too.

What Peter did before the crucifixion

Peter boasted that he would die for Jesus. Jesus told Peter that instead he would deny him. When Jesus was arrested Peter took out his sword and struck off the ear of one of the high priest's servants. Jesus rebuked Peter and healed the man's ear. At the chief priest's house Peter denied Jesus. When Peter realised what he had done he ran away and cried bitterly.

What Peter did after the resurrection

After the resurrection Peter was the first to run into the empty tomb. Later when he realised that the man on the beach was Jesus he was the first into the water to get ashore. Jesus asked Peter if he truly loved him. Peter replied, 'Yes Lord, you know that I love you.' Jesus said, 'Feed my lambs.' When he responded to the same question again, Jesus told him 'Take care of my sheep.' When Jesus asked Peter for the third time, 'Do you love me?' Peter replied, 'Lord you know all things; you know that I love you.'

Jesus told him to feed his sheep. Jesus was telling Peter to look after believers, to teach them and help them to follow Christ. Jesus then said to Peter, 'Follow me!'

What Jesus wants us to learn from the life of Peter

Despite our mistakes and our sin Jesus forgives. He knows what we are like and if we love him or not. We cannot hide anything from him. Jesus knew that Peter would deny him, but he also knew that Peter loved him. Jesus took Peter back and gave him an important job to do. Christians today must also love Christ and work for him.

BIBLE DATA 018

Read John 18:15-27. Do you remember what Peter was like at the chief priest's house? What happened to Peter after Jesus went back to heaven? Read Acts 4:13 and 20.

Pilate the Roman Governor

SCRIPTURE LOCATION: Matthew 27; Mark 15; Luke 3, 13, 23; John 19;

LINK BACK: Pages 48-53; 59; 61; 72

Who was Pilate?

Pilate was the Roman governor of Judea. He commanded the region's military forces and was responsible for issuing the death penalty. Pilate was a ruthless commander and was even responsible for slaughtering a group of Jews during an act of worship. However he didn't always stand up for what he believed in.

Pilate and Jesus

When Jesus was brought to Pilate he didn't want to sentence him to death. When Pilate heard Jesus say he was the Son of God this frightened him and he said to Jesus, 'Don't you realise that I have the power either to free you or to crucify you?'

Jesus replied, 'You would have no power over me if it were not given to you from above. Therefore the one who handed me over to you is guilty of a greater sin.'

Pilate again tried to free Jesus but the religious leaders accused Pilate of being an enemy of Caesar. Pilate then gave the crowd the choice between Jesus or a famous murderer. The crowd chose the murderer, Barabbas. Pilate then ordered that Jesus be whipped but the crowd still called out for Jesus to be crucified.

Pilate's wife warned her husband not to have anything to do with Jesus. She had had a bad dream and knew that Jesus was innocent. However Pilate did not listen to her and gave in to the demands of the priests. As he did so he took some water and washed his hands in front of the crowd. 'I am innocent of this man's blood,' he said. 'It is your responsibility.'

Pilate let the priests bully him into crucifying Jesus. He tried to make it look as though it was not his fault. Pilate sinned in what he did.

What does Jesus want us to learn from the life of Pilate?

Jesus said to Pilate, 'I came into the world to testify to the truth. Everyone on the side of the truth listens to me.' Pilate asked the question, 'What is truth?' Jesus Christ is truth. Jesus Christ himself says, 'I am the way, the truth and the life,' John 14:6. When we believe in Jesus we will have the courage to stand up for the truth. Pilate did not believe in Jesus so he did not have this courage.

FILE 036/ROMAN CENTURIONS

A centurion, was a Roman commander who had 100 soldiers under his command. The centurions followed Pilate's orders and whipped Jesus. They dressed him in a purple robe and placed a crown of thorns on his head. They made fun of him, spat on him and beat him. They nailed him to the cross and while Jesus was suffering they played a game to see who would win Jesus' clothes.

BIBLE DATA 019

A centurion asked Jesus to heal his servant. Read Luke 7:1-10. What did he say in verse 6? What did Jesus say about the centurion? A centurion saw Jesus die on the cross. Read Mark 15:39. What did he say about Jesus? What should we learn from these centurions?

The Pharisees

SCRIPTURE LOCATION: Matthew 12, 22, 23, 27, 28; John 18

LINK BACK: Pages 58-59; 70; 85; 44-45

Pharisees

Many people were against Jesus. They didn't like to hear the truth. Jesus spoke bluntly to his enemies about their sins. Pharisees thought they were better than everyone else. They were religious Jewish men who wanted to keep the Jewish laws. They made up their own rules and thought that they were as important as God's rules.

The Pharisees and Jesus

When Jesus healed people on the Sabbath, the Jewish holy day, the Pharisees said that this was unlawful. Jesus told them that it was lawful to do good on the Sabbath. This angered the Pharisees so much that they started plotting how they would kill Jesus. Jesus criticised them for telling others to keep a list of laws that they couldn't keep themselves.

How do we please God?

Pleasing God is not about keeping a list of rules. Pleasing God is about believing in his Son whom he loves. The Pharisees tried to keep lots of laws but they despised other people and they did not love Jesus. They did not really know how to please God or be holy at all.

What does Jesus want us to learn from the Pharisees?

Jesus wants us to remember that our God is a loving God who is a caring and forgiving Father. The Pharisees were not caring. They were often spiteful and critical of other people. The Pharisees didn't think they needed to ask God for forgiveness. Jesus was kind and loving to those he met.

INFORMATION SPOT

To find out more facts about the Pharisees turn to pages 44-45; 58-59; 85; 88.

BIBLE DATA 020

Read Luke 18:9-14. Who tried to exalt himself and who humbled himself? What should we do? Here is an instruction that Jesus gave the Pharisees. 'Learn what this means: "I desire mercy, not sacrifice." For I have not come to call the righteous but sinners.' What verse in Hosea 6 was Jesus was quoting from.

Judas Iscariot

Judas the thief

Judas was one of the twelve disciples chosen by Jesus. He was with Jesus for about three years. He would have seen Jesus' miracles and heard him preach. Judas was the treasurer for the disciples and Jesus. What little money they had was under Judas' care to hand out as it was needed. However Judas stole from the funds.

Judas the betrayer

One day Judas went to the chief priests to betray Jesus. The priests promised to give him money as a reward. From that moment Judas was on the look out for the right time to betray the Lord. Then one evening Judas lead some soldiers and religious officials to the Garden of Gethsemane where Jesus had been praying. He took the soldiers to the garden and then went to kiss Jesus. A kiss was used as a friendly greeting in Bible times, or as a sign of respect. Judas used it to show Jesus' enemies who to arrest.

Judas' death

Jesus was arrested and taken away. After that Judas was filled with guilt over his actions. He returned to the religious leaders and threw their money on the floor. He then went and killed himself. The priests could not use the money in the temple as it had been used to send Jesus to his death. So instead they used the money to purchase a piece of land called, The Potter's field, that would be used as a burial place for foreigners. Even this action by the priests fulfilled one of the prophecies from the Old Testament from the book of Jeremiah where it was prophesied that a field would be bought for thirty pieces of silver, the price that the people of Israel had set on the Messiah, the Lord Jesus Christ. In the book of Acts you can read about how a new disciple was chosen to take Judas' place.

What does Jesus want us to learn from the life of Judas Iscariot?

Judas spent his time around Jesus and with the other disciples - this did not make him right with God. Judas still rejected Jesus and betrayed him. Judas let his love of money persuade him to betray the Son of God.

If you spend time with God's people and have been taught the word of God do not reject Jesus as this is a very shameful thing to do. People who are brought up to learn about Jesus should believe the word that they have heard and not ignore it.

BIBLE DATA 021

Read Psalm 41:9 and 109:6. David talks about someone who betrayed him but this verse is also a prophecy about what would happen to Jesus. Read Zechariah 11:12. A prophecy is made regarding the silver that Judas was paid for betraying Jesus. What amount is mentioned?

The birth of Christ

The baby Jesus

If you wanted to make sure that people would listen to your message what would you do? Would you send a wise man who knew lots of things? Would you send someone who could tell the future? Perhaps you would send an important king with thousands of soldiers? Would you send a baby? God did. God sent his own Son as a helpless infant. The baby Jesus needed to be fed, cleaned and looked after. He needed parents to bring him up.

The child Jesus

Jesus lived his life just as we do except that he never sinned. Jesus ate and slept and did everything just as you and I do. He was a young child, a teenager and grew up to be a man.

Jesus is God and man

Jesus shows us how to live. He lived the perfect life instead of us. He shows us all how to live. His perfect life and then his death on the cross mean that people of all ages can be saved from sin. Jesus knows what it is like to be human – he knows what it is like to be tired, he knows what it is like to suffer. He understands you – whatever age you are.

Jesus is God's Son

God didn't just send us a prophet who could tell us what the future will bring. God didn't just send a wise man or a priest who knew lots of things. He didn't just send an important king. He sent us a baby – who was a prophet, priest and king. God the Father sent God the Son.

Jesus is our prophet, priest and king

Jesus Christ is our prophet, he holds the future in his hands and knows the end from the beginning. Jesus Christ is our priest. He has direct access to God the Father on our behalf. He is the Son of God. We can speak directly to God through Jesus Christ.

Jesus Christ is the King of Kings. He rules the earth and heavens and God's Kingdom will never end.

INFORMATION SPOT

For more information on the birth of Jesus turn to pages 8-15.

BIBLE DATA 022

Jesus Christ was truly human. Read Matthew 26:37; Luke 2:40; Luke 4:2; Luke 8:23; Luke 9:58; Luke 24:39 and John 4:6. How do these verses show us that Jesus Christ is human, just as we are, yet without sin?

The death of Christ

SCRIPTURE LOCATION: matthew 27; mark 15; Luke 23; John 19

LINK BACK: Pages 48-59; 78-79

Who is responsible?

This is an interesting question. You could give several answers to it. Here are a few:

The Jewish authorities

The religious leaders plotted to kill Christ. They gave money to Judas and they approached the Roman authorities.

The Roman authorities

Jesus was sentenced to death by the Roman authorities, on the orders of Pilate. However, Pilate thought that Jesus was innocent and tried to release him.

Judas Iscariot

Although Judas regretted his actions later and returned the money, he did accept money in payment for his betrayal of Christ and led the authorities to Jesus.

Jesus Christ

On several occasions Jesus Christ mentioned the fact that he would die. He even mentioned details connected to his death. During his trial when he was asked specific questions he remained silent. Jesus could have escaped crucifixion. Instead he went willingly to die on the cross. Jesus knew that his death would save God's people from their sins.

The Lord God

God the Father sent his Son to die on the cross because he loved the world. 'For God so loved the world that he gave his one and only son that whoever believes in him should not perish but have everlasting life,' John 3:16.

You and your sin

All of us are sinners and have rejected God. It should have been us who suffered the full anger of God. Jesus suffered and died in our place. It was our sin and our wrong doing that sent Jesus to the cross.

INFORMATION SPOT

Link this study back to the story of Jesus' birth by reading up on the gifts that the wise men brought to the young child Jesus. Which gift could have foretold his death? Which gift foretold his authority and kingship and which gift foretold his spiritual role? Turn to pages 14-15.

The resurrection of Christ

SCRIPTURE LOCATION: Matthew 28; Mark 16; Luke 24; John 20 and 21

LINK BACK: Pages 40-41; 59; 60-61; 98

How did it happen?

The power of God raised Jesus from the dead. His body had been buried in a tomb and had been dead three days when he rose again.

It is important for us to believe in the resurrection of Jesus Christ from the dead. Paul says in 1 Corinthians 15:17 'If Christ has not been raised your faith is futile and you are still in your sins.'

Jesus' enemies still tried to stop the truth by lying. They said that Jesus' disciples stole his body. But this lie could not stop the truth. People saw the Lord Jesus for themselves - hundreds of them. Because of the amazing truth of Jesus' resurrection the disciples stopped being frightened cowards and became bold preachers. Even when they were beaten for following Jesus none of them turned away from the truth. They knew that Jesus was alive and with his Father in heaven.

Why did Jesus rise from the dead?

Jesus' resurrection proves that he is God. We can now know that our bodies too will be raised back to life as God has promised. The resurrection shows us that Jesus Christ has defeated death and hell.

Our own resurrection

At the end of time the bodies of believers and unbelievers will be brought back to life. Those who believe in Christ will be raised again to live an eternal life, and those who did not believe in Christ will be raised again to punishment. The bodies of believers will be glorious and powerful. When we see Jesus we shall be like him.

Resurrection and the Old Testament

These verses in the Old Testament refer to the resurrection at the end of time.

'And after my skin is destroyed, this I know, that in my flesh I shall see God,' Job 19:26.

'Your dead will live; their bodies will rise,' Isaiah 26:19.

'Multitudes who sleep in the dust of the earth will awake: some to everlasting life, others to shame and everlasting contempt,' Daniel 12:2.

'You will not abandon me to the grave, nor will you let your Holy One see decay,' Psalm 16:10.

We can be certain that Jesus Christ is alive today. The Bible says so. We can always trust God's word. It is true.

Study section

FOR: Personal or group studies

THEMES: God's love; God's power; salvation; Jesus; Pleasing God; The Bible

Bible data answers

PURPOSE: Bible Data answers are found throughout this book. Their purpose is to help you discover the bible for yourself.

BIBLE DATA 001

Isaiah 9:1, 42:6, 49:6 and 22; Matthew 28:19

Jesus tells his followers to go into all the world to preach the news of Jesus and salvation. This is a commandment to all Jesus' followers then and now.

BIBLE DATA 002

Hebrews 4:15; 1 John 1:8; Romans 3:23

Jesus has no sin. If we say we have no sin we deceive ourselves as all have sinned.

BIBLE DATA 003

Mark 14:38; Luke 22:40; 1 Corinthians 10:13

We are to pray so we don't fall into temptation. The temptations we face will not be too difficult to resist. Whatever we face God will help us and give us a way out of it.

BIBLE DATA 004

Mark 15:33-39

The centurion at the cross exclaimed, 'Truly this is the son of God.'

BIBLE DATA 005

Matthew 17:5; James 1:19

God the Father told people to listen to his beloved Son, Jesus. We are told to be quick to listen, slow to speak and slow to become angry.

BIBLE DATA 006

Matthew 14:1-12

King Herod made the mistake of thinking that Jesus Christ might actually be John the Baptist come back to life. Herod had executed John the Baptist earlier on.

BIBLE DATA 007

1 Corinthians 11:23-28

We are to celebrate the Lord's supper to remember Jesus' death for us. Beforehand we should see what in our lives upsets God, and ask God to forgive and help us.

BIBLE DATA 008

2 Timothy 3:12; John 15:18

Believers in Jesus Christ will be persecuted. Any who want to please God will be persecuted. Jesus reminds his people that the world will hate them because it hated him first. We should pray for those who persecute us and bless them too. Jesus prayed for his murderers, 'Father forgive them for they don't know what they are doing.'

BIBLE DATA 009

John 21:25

In this verse John tells us that Jesus did lots of things - and that if every one of them was written down in a book the whole world wouldn't be big enough for all of them.

BIBLE DATA 010

Matthew 6:27-34; Matthew 28 – 20

These verses tell us not to worry about the future and that Jesus will be with us always even to the very end of the world.

Bible Data answers
continued

PURPOSE: Bible Data Answers are found throughout this book. Their purpose is to help you discover the bible for yourself.

BIBLE DATA 011

Isaiah 9:1-2

Where did Jesus perform many miracles? Galilee. Where was he baptised? Jordan. What two words are mentioned in Isaiah 9:2 and John 8:12: darkness and light.

BIBLE DATA 012

Psalm 22:1; Mark 15:34.

The words 'My God, My God why have you forsaken me?' appear in both verses.

BIBLE DATA 013

Luke 24; 1 Corinthians 1:18

In 1 Corinthians 1:18 we are told something amazing about God's power. The word of the Cross or the truth of Christ dying for us is powerful. It saves us from our sin.

BIBLE DATA 014

Matthew 4:18-22, 8:18-22, 9:9-12, 11:20-24, 12:1-8, 15:21-28, 19:13-15; Luke 7:36-50, 19:1-10; John 3:1-21

Jesus spoke with fishermen, tax collectors, sinners, women, men, children, religious leaders, people who loved him, people who didn't.

BIBLE DATA 015

1John 4:14; Romans 6: 23, 10:13; Acts 4:10-12; Isaiah 55:1; Rev 5:9

God the Father sent Jesus. All who call to the Lord for help can obtain salvation. It is only found through Christ, it costs nothing. It is a gift from God, but it cost Jesus his life.

BIBLE DATA 016

Matthew 1; Luke 3; Romans 1:3; 1 Timothy 6:15; 2 Timothy 2:8

Jesus is the King of Kings who rose from the dead. David died as everyone does.

BIBLE DATA 017

John 1:19-23; Isaiah 40:3

John the Baptist said Jesus was the Messiah and that he was not worthy to untie Jesus' sandals. He prepared the way for Jesus. Isaiah 40:3 should remind us of John 1:23.

BIBLE DATA 018

John 18:15-27; Acts 4:13; Acts 4:20

Peter was a coward and denied Jesus. After Jesus went back to heaven Peter became bold and he would not stop speaking about the things he had seen and heard.

BIBLE DATA 019

Luke 7:1-10; Mark 15:39

The centurion said 'I do not deserve to have you under my roof.' Jesus said 'I have not seen such great faith even in Israel.' The centurion at the cross said, 'Surely this man was the Son of God.' They teach us to be humble with Jesus and to believe in him.

BIBLE DATA 020

Luke 18:9-14

The pharisee exalted himself; the tax-collector humbled himself. We should be humble too. Hosea 6:6 is the verse Jesus quotes 'I desire mercy, not sacrifice.'

BIBLE DATA 021

Psalm 41:9; Psalm 109:6; Zechariah 11:12

Zechariah 11:12 prophesies about the silver that Judas would be paid: thirty pieces.

BIBLE DATA 022

Matthew 26:37; Luke 2:40, 4:2, 8:23, 9:58, 24:39; John 4:6

Matthew 26:37, Jesus suffered sorrow; Luke 2:40, Jesus grew up physically; Luke 4:2, Jesus was hungry; Luke 8:23, Jesus fell asleep; Luke 9:58 Jesus was poor; Luke 24:39, Jesus has a physical body and John 4:6, Jesus got weary.

EXTRA FEATURE

General Index

PURPOSE: An aid to study or to help you find out where to look up a topic, place, or person.

Published by

 **CHRISTIAN FOCUS**

Christian Focus Publications publishes books for adults and children
under its three main imprints: Christian Focus, Mentor and Christian Heritage.
Our books reflect that God's word is reliable and Jesus is the way to know him,
and live for ever with him.

Our children's publication list includes a Sunday school curriculum
that covers pre-school to early teens; puzzle and activity books.
We also publish personal and family devotional titles,
biographies and inspirational stories that children will love.

If you are looking for quality Bible teaching for children
then we have an excellent range of Bible story
and age specific theological books.

From pre-school to teenage fiction, we have it covered!

Find us at our web page:
www.christianfocus.com